RAILWAYS
FOR
PLEASURE

THE COMPLETE GUIDE TO STEAM
AND SCENIC LINES IN GREAT BRITAIN
AND IRELAND

KENNETH WESTCOTT JONES

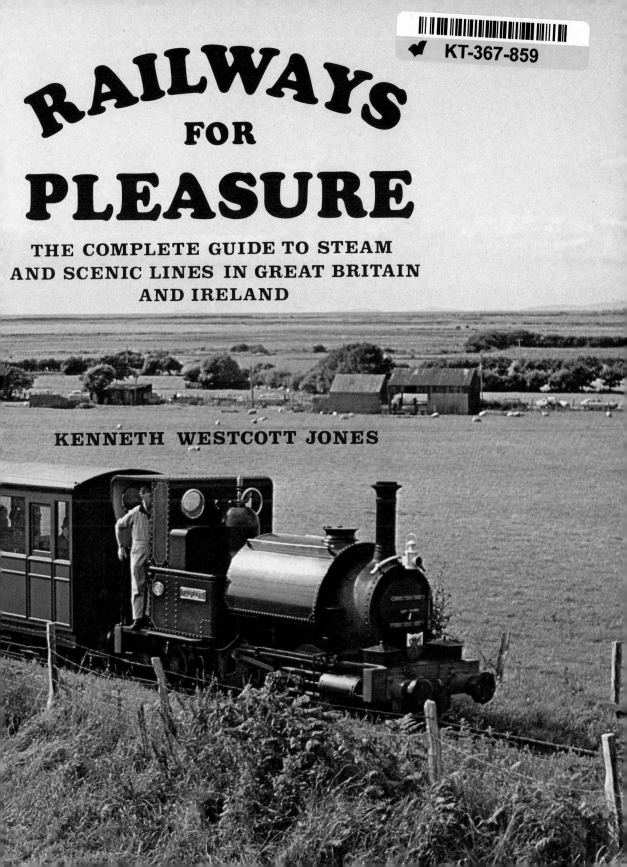

First published in Great Britain by
Lutterworth Press, Guildford & London,
in 1980

Copyright © 1980 Ventura Publishing
Ltd, London

Created, designed and produced by
Ventura Publishing Ltd, 44 Uxbridge
Street, London W8 7TG

ISBN Cased: 0 7188 2467 9
       Paper: 0 7188 2446 6

Filmset in Great Britain by SX Composing
Ltd, Rayleigh, Essex

Colour origination by Colour Workshop
Ltd, Hertford, Herts

Printed and bound in Singapore

Frontispiece: Talyllyn Railway

Front cover: Keighley and Worth Valley
Railway
Back cover: Ravenglass and Eskdale
Railway
(Photos by Mike Esau; Yorkshire and
Humberside Tourist Board; Nick Stanbra)

The publishers have made every effort to
ensure that the information in this book
is correct at the time of going to press,
March 1980.
Any correspondence concerned with the
contents of this volume should be
addressed to Ventura Publishing Ltd,
44 Uxbridge St, London W8.

Contents

6

Railways For Pleasure
Key to entries in order of
appearance in the book

1 London and the South-East

2 The South and West

3 Wales

4 The Midlands and East Anglia

5 The North

6 Scotland

7 Ireland

British Rail Scenic Lines

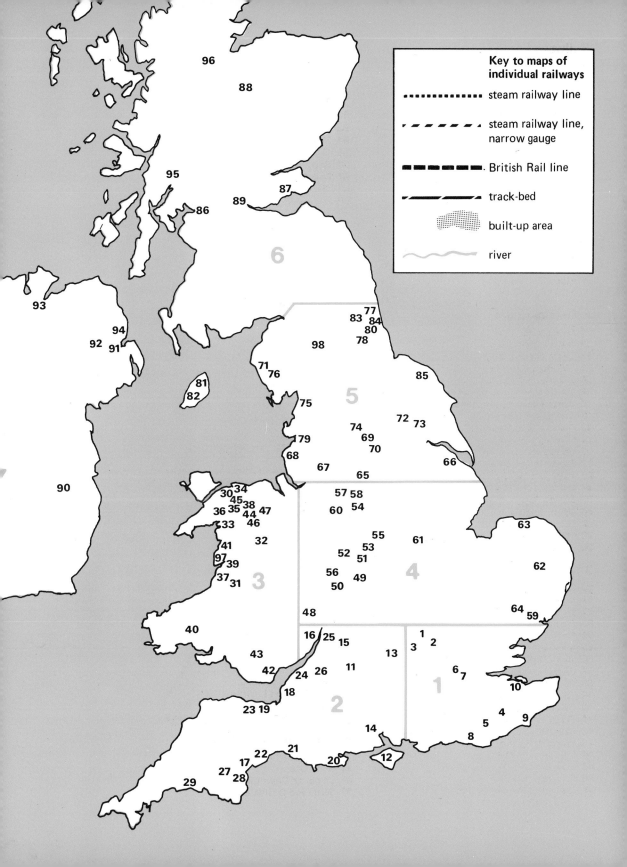

Key to maps of individual railways

········· steam railway line

⫻⫻⫻⫻⫻ steam railway line, narrow gauge

▬ ▬ ▬ ▬ British Rail line

⟋⟋⟋⟋ track-bed

⣿⣿⣿ built-up area

〜〜〜 river

Foreword by Alan Pegler

President, Festiniog Railway Company and President, Festiniog Railway Society Limited

Time and again attempts have been made to try and explain the magic of steam, particularly as applied to railway locomotives. Just what is it that has such a strong appeal for so many people and yet leaves a few quite unmoved? On the whole, steam locomotives were designed as handsome machines. In Great Britain, unlike many other countries, it was usual for them to be painted in a variety of colours in addition to the traditional black and very fine most of them looked.

Today there are many museums around the country where immaculately preserved steam locomotives may be seen at close quarters and in 1978 British Rail themselves started running steam hauled special trains. Here, perhaps, is the first positive clue to the source of the sheer delight of the steam locomotive – the difference between one which is standing spotless in a museum and one which has a fire in its belly and is out 'on the road'.

In some ways the two bases from which the 1978 and 1979 British Rail steam specials were run provide an extension to this line of thought. York, which inaugurated the Circular Tours via Leeds and Harrogate, is also the home of the National Railway Museum; a superb museum it is, too. Carnforth, which has been responsible for turning out the locomotives which worked the Cumbrian Coast and North Yorkshireman excursions, is a steam depot as well as a museum and the accent is on having main line locomotives there in a good serviceable condition. Apart from clean floors and central heating at York as opposed to the inevitable quota of grime underfoot and often a cold draught when the shed doors are open at Carnforth, what is the thing that strikes the reasonable observer about these two admirable institutions? So far as I am concerned, it's the smell.

A locomotive which is in immaculate condition has a lot of its surplus grease and oil removed whereas one which is kept in a cold shed, where other movements are going on nearly all the time, will of necessity have pretty liberal coatings of grease in evidence. This, mixed with whiffs of soot, produces something which is so characteristic as to be unique. However, this is nothing compared with the smell when the fire has been lit and the whole locomotive gets warm and this, in turn, gives many of us that heady delight of the smell of a steam train after it has gone by. One stands and waits for the train to approach and one hears the first sound of it in the distance, then there is the thrill of seeing it as it approaches and thunders past and finally – sometimes for a long time afterwards – that nostalgic smell lingers on.

Lord Beeching, in a magazine interview in 1979, said he couldn't 'get all worked up about a piece of ironmongery'. On the same occasion he went on record as saying 'there's no room for false sentiment about the inanimate' and concluded by declaring that he would rather have a pub named after him than a locomotive. I suggest that not many of us share those views and if that is the case this book by Kenneth Westcott Jones will bring tremendous satisfaction to the illogical majority of which I am happy to call myself a member. If you, like me, love the sight, sound and smell of steam locomotives you will find within these pages just about every variety; miniature, narrow gauge, standard gauge and main line. Enormous amounts of effort and money have been spent on preserving this part of our heritage and the cost of maintenance is going up all the time. What these centres now need is the continuing support of the public, particularly in the shape of paying visitors or fare-paying passengers. This book will help you plan visits which will ensure that support and give you pleasure at the same time. Here's to happy steaming in the '80s and beyond!

Members of the Mid-Hants Railway locomotive group spent 30,000 hours of their spare time restoring this locomotive *Bodmin*.

Acknowledgements

The author and publishers are most grateful for all the assistance they have received in compiling this book. They would particularly like to thank all the railways, museums, centres and preservation societies who kindly provided photographs and gave permission to reproduce them. Also Dennis Joiner, Chief Press Officer of the British Railways Board, for his help. Individual photographers are acknowledged, as far as possible, on the following list. Otherwise, the source of the photograph is listed.

Stephen Edge: 1, 48, 49; Tony Hudson: 14, 27 (below), 71 (centre and bottom), 90, 91; Mid-Hants 'Watercress' Line: 11; G. A. Barlow: 16; J. Horsley: 20; I. K. Hutchinson: 21 (top); Mervyn Leah: 21 (centre and bottom); Whipsnade and Umfolozi Railway: 22 (top); K. A. Lane: 22 (bottom); A. Lyster: 23; Mike Esau: 3, 26, 27; Chris Mitchell: 24, 25; Brighton Borough Council: 29; Romney, Hythe and Dymchurch Railway: 30, 31; John Goss: 37 (top and centre); Peter Relf: 37 (bottom); C. F. D. Whetmath: 38 (top and bottom), 39 (bottom); P. Treloar 39 (centre); Ian Crowder: 40, 41; P. Skinner: 42; F. Scoon: 43 (bottom); 'Gloucester Citizen': 43 (top); East Somerset Railway: 44; A. J. Morgan: 45; Eastbourne Public Relations Department: 46 (centre and bottom right); Bicton Woodland Railway: 47 (bottom left); Dowty Railway Preservation Society: 50; Bitton Railway Centre 51; J. Besley: 52 (centre); Tim Stephens: 52 (bottom); Roger Penny: 54 (top); Nicholas Home: 55; P. Zabek: 56 (top); L. A. Nixon: 56 (bottom); Forest Railroad Park: 57; J. F. Rimmer: 60, 74 (bottom), 75, 76, 78, 89 (top); A. Robey: 62; Welshpool and Llanfair Railway: 64; R. I. Cartwright: 65; D. H. Wilson: 66 (far right); Robin Ellis: 67 (top left); Festiniog Railway: 67 (bottom); Llandudno Urban District Council: 69; Welsh Highland Light Railway: 72, 73; P. G. Wright: 77; Llechwedd Slate Caverns: 81; D. A. Burns: 85; Llangollen Railway Society: 84; Colourviews: 89 (bottom); Cadeby Light Railway: 93; Midland Railway Centre: 94, 95; Martin Gadsby: 98; A. D. Packer: 99; Stour Valley Railway Preservation Society: 100 (top); G. D. King: 100 (centre and bottom); Nene Valley Railway: 102, 103; Bressingham Steam Museum: 104; Brian Fisher: 106, 107 (top and centre); M. Sales: 107 (bottom); H. Parrish: 110, 111; Steamport Southport: 113; Middleton Railway Trust Collection: 116, 117 (top right and bottom); A. P. Bell: 117 (top); Nick Stanbra: 119, J. R. Ellis: 122 (top), 123 (top and bottom right); R. O. Coffin: 124; T. Boustead: 125 (top); T. G. Lodge: 127; Manx Press Pictures: 130, 133 (top right); Isle of Man Railways: 131 (top), 132, 133; North Yorkshire Moors Railway: 136, 137 (top); Ian Addison: 140; P. Westwater: 141; Bill Roberton: 142, 143; Shane's Castle Light Railway: 146, 148, 149.

They would like to thank the following organisations for permission to reproduce photographs: British Rail: 125 (bottom), 139, 151, 157; British Tourist Authority: 79 (top), 81, 97, 120, 128, 156; South-East England Tourist Board: 34, 35; West Country Tourist Board: 46 (bottom right), 53; Wales Tourist Board: 63, 66, 67 (top right), 70, 71 (top), 79 (bottom), 82, 83; Yorkshire and Humberside Tourist Board: front and back cover, 114, 115, 121, 128, 137; National Trust: 61; Scottish Tourist Board: 139 (centre and bottom), 144, 153; The Times: 28.

They are very grateful to the Romney, Hythe and Dymchurch Railway, Mid-Hants 'Watercress' Line, Welshpool and Llanfair Railway, Festiniog Railway, Talyllyn Railway, and Llechwedd Slate Caverns, for permission to use their railway letter stamps.

Thanks also go to all those who worked on the production of the book: Gwyn Lewis for the design of the book; Stuart Perry for the map of Great Britain and Ireland and the individual railway maps; Richard Fowler for the area maps; and Jackie Fortey for editing and research.

Preface

The centres described in this book are all open to the public at prescribed times, and none of them requires special permission for a visit. A few are free, most cost money, but it must be remembered that steam train rides are expensive to arrange, even allowing for dedicated work by volunteers. Fares charged should not be measured on a mileage basis, but for the interest and enjoyment the journey affords. Advance bookings are not required.

In most cases the centres provide good car parking, which is usually free. Children are welcomed, and should be brought to sample this form of traction. It will help to impress upon them the importance of the steam engine as the major breakthrough in the development of transport and its immense contribution to Britain's greatness, following her lead at the time of the Industrial Revolution.

Refreshment rooms are part and parcel of most preserved lines and steam centres. Prices are kept to a modest level, the small profit being put to excellent use on the railway. I do not know of any café or refreshment room on a preserved railway staffed other than by willing volunteers.

The shops mentioned in the text are well stocked with railway books, guides to the particular line, postcards, souvenir items such as cups and mugs with locomotive designs on them, jigsaw puzzles of trains, tea towels, pens, paintings, pennants, ashtrays, key rings, and often railway models. They are all worthy of support, even a modest purchase, such as a pair of balloons decorated with steam engines, contributing something to the high cost of running a preserved railway.

By purchasing a ticket to ride and using the facilities, the reader will avoid that curious accusation of being a 'Gricer'. This is a recent term, widely used in English speaking lands, and its exact meaning is not clear, but one is a 'Gricer' who drives to a preserved steam line, chases trains with a car, photographs them, and spends nothing on the railway.

Whyte's Formula

Devised over a century ago to describe the wheel arrangements for steam locomotives, Whyte's Formula is in use throughout the former British Empire and Commonwealth and the United States, also South America and Japan. In France and most other Continental countries a different (lettered) system applies. With the Whyte method, leading (bogie) wheels are shown followed by driving wheels, then trailing wheels, ON BOTH SIDES, a zero being shown if there are no bogies or trailers.

0–4–0, 2–4–0, 2–4–2, 4–4–0.
4–4–2 (known as 'Atlantics').

4–4–4, 2–4–4, 0–6–0, 0–6–2.
2–6–0 (Mogul).
2–6–2 (Prairie).
2–6–4, 4–6–0, 4–6–2 (Pacific).
4–6–4 (Baltic).
0–8–0, 2–8–0 (Consolidation).
2–8–2 (Mikado).
4–8–0, 4–8–2 (Mountain).
4–8–4 (Northern).
0–10–0 (Decapod).
2–10–0.

Tank engines are indicated by the letter T, saddle tanks by ST, well tanks by WT, and pannier tanks by PT.

Introduction

Catering for the intense nostalgia British people, especially men, feel for vintage railways and steam traction, an industry has developed during the past 30 years. To say it is a growth industry is an understatement, for preserved railways and steam museums and steam centres have become a vitally important part of our lives, spreading the length and breadth of the land.

If this book had been written in 1952 it would have been a very slim volume indeed, containing one major railway museum (the original structure at York), one working steam railway (the Talyllyn, first preserved line in the world), and perhaps some oddities such as Volks Electric and the Bridgnorth Cliff Railway. Instead, it appears in 1980 with no less than 98 entries, and even this total does not include a few projects which will shortly show promise.

It is the established policy of the English Tourist Board – a Government-funded body required to develop visitor attractions in this country – that no family should be more than 50 miles from a steam railway. It is officially hoped that no child will grow up without having been taken to experience a steam train ride, and to further this aim several steam railways and rail museums have been grant-aided.

Steam traction on British Railways ended in August 1968, several years ahead of the date anticipated by the White Paper, published in 1955, which set out modernisation proposals. The original intention was to phase out steam engines over a period of 20 years, replacing them with 'stop-gap' diesels and electrification. Instead of various types of diesel locomotives being tested in order to determine a very limited number of standard and effective types for quantity production, hundreds of poor quality ones flooded the system, some of them junk on wheels which had very brief and expensive lives. Their coming destroyed vast fleets of steam engines with decades of worthwhile service still left in them. Steam nostalgia grew rapidly as a result.

The Beeching era, saddest and cruellest period of rail administration Britain – and most other countries – had ever known,

Crowds admire ex-GNR 4–4–2 No. 990 *Henry Oakley* at Shildon in 1975.

cut back the size of the system. More and more steam engines were left with no work to do and they went early to the scrapyards.

Management following in the wake of Beeching denigrated steam, the subsequent Chairman, Stanley Raymond, going so far as to say, late in 1965, that as soon as British Railways had got rid of its last steam engine, deficits would end. The only three remaining on the system after mid-August, 1968, were the three narrow gauge engines which continue to give such pleasure to riders of the Vale of Rheidol Railway in Wales. One has to presume, if the Chairman's remark was fact, that each locomotive lost British Railways more than £30 millions in 1969 and 1970!

The continued scorn poured upon steam had the effect of increasing steam nostalgia among enthusiasts, and contributed to the proliferation of preserved lines. Engines were saved from the Woodhams scrap yards at Barry and restored with public subscriptions. At that period, British Railways management obstructed every move, sometimes setting impossible prices upon short rusting lengths of track and fixing abrupt deadlines for the raising of huge sums. Bridges and vital junctions were demolished overnight, the effect of these moves still restricting operations on the isolated Bluebell Line and the Dart Valley to this day. But the uphill struggle continued, despite a total ban on the use of steam engines on the metals of British Railways. This was defied only by the stalwart Mr Alan Pegler who had bought

Flying Scotsman with a clause in his contract allowing him to run the engine for a number of years. In 1969, *Flying Scotsman* was taken on an operationally successful but financially disastrous visit to North America, which bankrupted Mr Pegler and finally cleared the State tracks of steam workings (apart from the Vale of Rheidol).

The preservation groups worked on, absurdly large sums of money being found to pay for derelict track, while all kinds of official obstacles were overcome. The steam ban, which had lasted seven years, was finally relaxed, thanks to the efforts of Mr Peter Prior of Bulmers and his supporters, who managed to restore *King George V* and to run her on a special to Swindon in October 1972. A 'Return to Steam' movement chaired by artist David Shepherd began to succeed.

Slowly at first but steadily, under the chairmanship of Sir Richard Marsh, British Railways Management grew more constructive. Belatedly a better atmosphere developed on the railways, and this began to affect the by now very numerous preservation societies. Certain steam engines in their possession, after rigorous checks, were allowed to run on State metals, a thousand miles of which were cleared for steam operations. When Sir Richard Marsh became chairman of the Newspaper Society, he was replaced at the British Railways Board by Sir Peter Parker, a warm personality with a known affection for steam as well as an overall 'feeling' for railways. By now, high speed trains had

A line up of locomotives with enthusiastic onlookers at Shildon.

TOP: The RH&DR's No. 3 *Southern Maid* meets her big sister *Flying Scotsman* at Tyseley Steam Centre, Birmingham.

RIGHT: *Flying Scotsman*, restored by Alan Pegler.

appeared, slashing journey times, while electrification had reached Scotland by the West Coast route. The 'junk' diesels had gone to scrapyards not long after the steam engines they were supposed to replace, and a standardized diesel (class 47) was succeeding.

A new breed of diesel enthusiasts had appeared, and a few classes, notably the withdrawn 'Western' class diesel hydraulics from Swindon, were popular. Like the steam engines before them, some were bought and put to work on the expanding preserved lines. But steam remained the key thing and interest continued to grow, contrary to the beliefs of the early 1960s.

By 1978, British Rail Management literally stated that 'if you can't beat them, join them'. British Rail began to run steam excursions of its own, re-steaming lines in the York, Leeds, Harrogate, Barrow and Carnforth areas, using either its own engines borrowed from the National Collection or hiring from preserved lines. At first on Sundays and then in mid-week, 'official' steam trains began to appear.

It is widely believed that the incredible turn-out by the public at Shildon for the privately organized 'Rail 150' cavalcade in August 1975, the greatest number of spectators for any event outside a Royal Coronation in London, was the turning point. It was clear that the 'steam bug' could not be put down, so it was decided to nourish it, gaining a spin-off in goodwill for the railways as a whole. For 'Rocket 150' events at Rainhill in 1980, British Rail has taken a leading part, arranging things and encouraging a large steam cavalcade. They have allocated no less than one million pounds for the occasion. Trains will even be operated behind steam for the whole of the summer of 1980 between Liverpool and Manchester at weekends.

There are probably about two million dedicated railway enthusiasts in Britain, the highest proportion to population in the world, although the United States (with 139 preserved steam railways) has more fans. Another two million people take more than a passing interest in railways, particularly steam trains, while many more who remember steam in regular use want their children to see and ride behind this form of traction. It is to that multitude this book is aimed, to guide them on family outings, so that they can enjoy some of the experiences a previous generation took for granted.

Wide choices of places to visit can be made all over England, Wales and Ireland, selecting railways passing through magnificent scenery, or unusual types of locomotive, or long runs which can actually be a useful journey. Excursions can be taken behind big steam engines out of Leeds and York and Barrow-in-Furness on a regular basis, using main line tracks and attaining that magic figure of 60 miles an hour. On special occasions, enthusiasts' outings can be joined which are advertised well in advance, with long runs behind specified locomotives from Newport to Crewe or even over the Pennines to Carlisle from Leeds (a route described in this book as among the scenic lines of British Rail).

Staffed, as most of them are, by volunteers (with perhaps one or two professional management) it is difficult to provide all year operations, and most activities are concentrated at holiday times, or at weekends.

A large population is needed to sustain preserved railways, which is why Scotland has so few of them. There is certainly room for one or two more, particularly in the Central Lowlands and it is expected that a short line from Falkirk to Bo'ness will soon be in action operated by the Scottish Railway Preservation Society. With supplies of petrol dwindling and its cost escalating, long drives in search of steam may not be easy or even possible in a few years time. It will be even more important that sufficient preserved steam railways are operating in various regions to enable visitors to reach them easily, especially by public transport.

Steam railways, thanks to the work of Talyllyn pioneers three decades ago, have a good future, and will undoubtedly steam into the 21st Century with coal fired engines puffing away even after the last drop of petroleum has been burned.

The return to steam: *King George V* with Bulmer's Pullman train at Kensington Olympia, about to leave for Swindon.

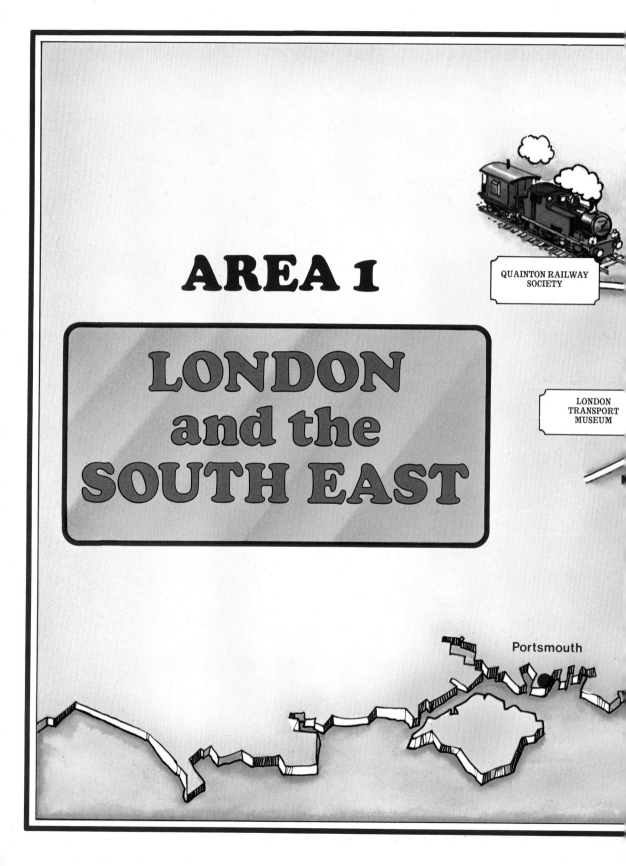

AREA 1

LONDON and the SOUTH EAST

QUAINTON RAILWAY SOCIETY

LONDON TRANSPORT MUSEUM

Portsmouth

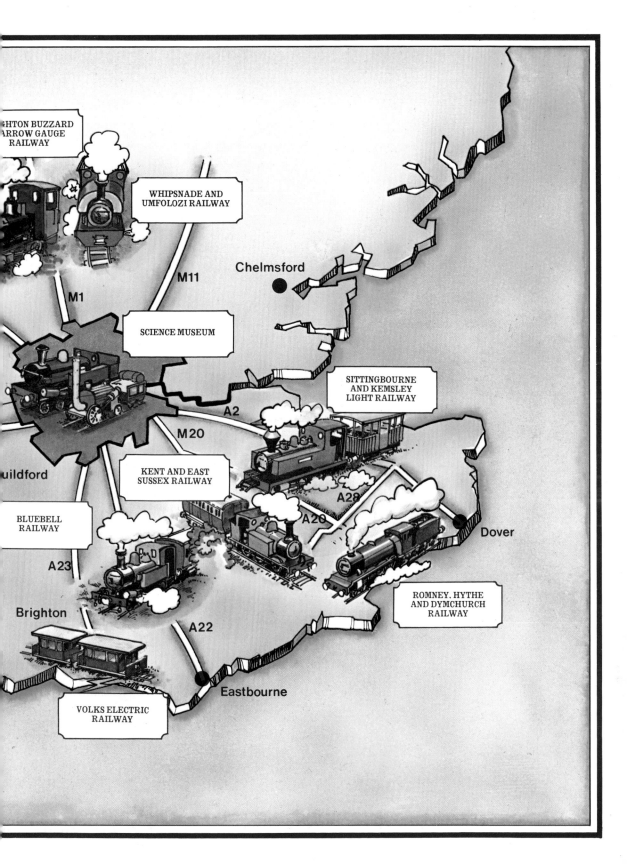

**HTON BUZZARD
ARROW GAUGE
RAILWAY**

**WHIPSNADE AND
UMFOLOZI RAILWAY**

M11

Chelmsford

M1

SCIENCE MUSEUM

**SITTINGBOURNE
AND KEMSLEY
LIGHT RAILWAY**

A2

M20

uildford

**KENT AND EAST
SUSSEX RAILWAY**

A28

A20

**BLUEBELL
RAILWAY**

Dover

A23

**ROMNEY, HYTHE
AND DYMCHURCH
RAILWAY**

Brighton

A22

Eastbourne

**VOLKS ELECTRIC
RAILWAY**

Leighton Buzzard Narrow Gauge Railway

The magic words Orenstein and Koppel are enough to bring the hard core of railway enthusiasts to the 2ft gauge light railway in Bedfordshire. For the less dedicated, who nevertheless enjoy pleasant chuffing rides on vintage trains, the Leighton Buzzard line (formerly the Sand Hutton Light Railway) offers a pleasant and unusual excursion.

Orenstein and Koppel were locomotive builders in Berlin specializing in narrow gauge steam tank engines capable of negotiating sharp curves and steep inclines. The four best examples in the world are on the Matheran Hill Railway some 50 miles inland from Bombay – a long way to go for the experience, though thousands of enthusiasts make the trip. Two of their well tanks can be seen at Leighton Buzzard. The 0–6–0 *Elf*, dating from 1936, was

found operating as a wood burner in Central Africa back in 1973 by a Mr A. Fisher. He rescued it and owns it now, allowing it to be employed among the Leighton Buzzard stock. An 0–4–0 *P.C. Allen* dates from 1912 and has a less dramatic history.

The Leighton Buzzard Narrow Gauge Railway Society Ltd, a registered charity and an industrial Friendly Society, is based at Page's Park station, Leighton Buzzard. Its tracks stretch for 3 miles to a place called Stonehenge (no connection with Salisbury Plain) but went on to the sand workings around Double Arches, 5 miles from Leighton Buzzard. There used to be a great deal of activity here during the two World Wars when silica sand was in huge demand. There is still some sand collection in this area.

BELOW RIGHT: Kerr Stuart 0–4–0 saddle tank *Pixie*, built in 1922.

LEFT: *Pixie* and her 'sister' *Peter Pan*.

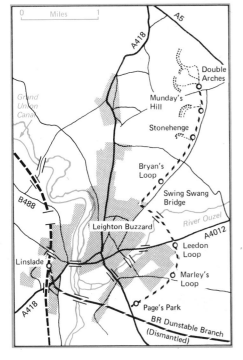

The ride terminates at Stonehenge, a trip of about 30 minutes each way. The engines and rolling stock are based at Page's Park. The remarkable little vertical boiler engine *Chaloner* – built in 1877 and said to be the oldest narrow gauge engine outside Wales – is at present on loan to the National Railway Museum, York. There are six steam engines and eight small diesels, plus seven coaches, some of them open-sided. One of the diesels is an Orenstein and Koppel from 1939.

Address Leighton Buzzard Narrow Gauge Railway Society Ltd, Page's Park Station, Billington Rd, Leighton Buzzard, Beds, LU7 8TN. Tel. Leighton Buzzard 373888

Enquiries to The Publicity Officer, at above address. Timetable available

Opening times 10.30–17.30, Sundays and Bank Holidays, April to September

How to get there *By road* A4146, ½ mile from town centre. *By rail* to Leighton Buzzard BR

Facilities Large car park, refreshment room, and a souvenir shop at Page's Park

Special attractions Off-peak fares before 14.30, after 16.30 and all day Saturday

Discounts For groups, available on application. Children half-price

TOP De Winton vertical boiler engine *Chaloner*, built in 1877 and one of the oldest working steam locomotives.

CENTRE Orenstein and Koppel well tank *P.C. Allen*, built in 1912, on the level crossing at Marley's Bank.

BELOW *P.C. Allen* climbing Marley's Bank with a train from Leedon.

Whipsnade and Umfolozi Railway

The attraction of Whipsnade Zoo, first of the great outdoor zoos in a natural setting, brings people to Dunstable, and they also normally enjoy a ride on this 2ft 6in gauge railway running through the animal paddocks.

It was purpose-built by Pleasurerail Ltd of London in 1970 as an extra attraction at the zoo and a safe means of viewing the larger animals at close range. The name Umfolozi was taken from the Zulu name of a north Natal game park. The railway operates over a circuit of some 3 miles, and there are steep gradients, sharp curves, even a tunnel. It is normally steam worked, using some of the steam engines and equipment from the Bowaters' Railway at Sittingbourne (surplus to the requirements of the Sittingbourne and Kemsley Light Railway), but with diesel traction on some mornings early and late in the season.

There are four steam engines, three diesels, a few works motor units and ten passenger coaches at the base station. In addition, a Class 7 Zambesi Sawmills 4–8–0 (3ft 6in gauge), owned by the artist, David Shepherd, is a static exhibit, with a clerestory carriage from the Rhodesian Railways.

Address Whipsnade and Umfolozi Railway, c/o Whipsnade Zoo, Dunstable, Beds. Tel. Whipsnade 872995

Enquiries to The Manageress, at above address

Opening times Daily, Easter to end September, school holidays and some weekends. Midday to 1 hr before zoo closes

How to get there *By road* via Whipsnade Park Zoo, south of Dunstable, off B4540. *By rail* to Luton BR

Facilities Car park, refreshments nearby

Special discounts For groups. Reduced rate for children

TOP RIGHT Kerr Stuart 0–4–2 saddle tank *Excelsior*.

BOTTOM RIGHT Bagnall 0–6–2 tank *Conqueror*, leaving the tunnel.

Quainton Railway Society

For people whose railway interest runs especially towards large displays of static locomotives and equipment, with the occasional chance to see some veterans in steam, Quainton Road Station, near Aylesbury, offers the largest outdoor collection.

In the old days, Quainton Road was a junction where the Great Central Railway and the Metropolitan Railway met and then continued towards London as a joint line, one of the last main line projects in Britain, built in 1899. It was 44 miles from London (Marylebone) and services ceased through the station with the closure of the Great Central north of Aylesbury in 1966.

The Quainton Railway Society, formed in 1968, shares the premises with the 6024 Preservation Society, the Ivatt Locomotive Trust, and the Great Central Railway Coach Group. In all they have thirty-three steam locomotives, the largest number of any organisation in this book, plus four diesels and twelve passenger coaches.

All the work is done by volunteers, but there is no distance 'run', although when engines are in steam on some summer weekends and at Bank Holidays, steam rides are given around yards and sidings.

Visitors will find much of interest if they have some knowledge of the pre-grouping railways. They are welcome to come at any weekend but there may be nothing happening beyond volunteers doing some restoration work.

The former GWR express locomotive *King Edward I*, No. 6024, bought by the 6024 preservation society, is now star attraction. Of particular note is a Metropolitan Railway 0–4–4 tank, built in 1896, a type once used on Aylesbury Line trains, and a participant in the Metropolitan Centenary parade of 1964. Two excellent Great Central Railway coaches are to be seen, a first class bogie of 1906 (the GCR had some of the finest rolling stock ever built in Britain) and an open third bogie from 1910. Some six-wheelers from the Great Northern, and even the Midland and South Western Junction, can be seen – ideal units for film-making if the period is the 1890s.

ABOVE LNWR first class kitchen/diner in undercoat with polished brass handles.

CENTRE LEFT Restoration work at Quainton.

BOTTOM LEFT The oldest Barclay in use in Britain, 0–4–0 saddle tank *Swanscombe* (1891), at Quainton for an Enthusiasts' Weekend.

Address Quainton Railway Society Ltd, Quainton Rd Station, Quainton, Aylesbury, Bucks.

Enquiries to Above address. Timetable available

Opening times Easter to end October, Sundays all year and Bank Holidays. Steaming, Bank Holiday weekends and last Sunday of month

How to get there *By road* Off A41 Aylesbury–Bicester. *By rail* to Aylesbury BR. Special diesel train Aylesbury to Quainton, Bank Holiday Mondays only

Facilities Ample car parking, good souvenir shop, refreshment room

Discounts For groups, by arrangement. Family tickets Bank Holiday weekends. Children half-price

Kent and East Sussex Railway

On the first of June 1974, a rare warm day, a crowd of well-wishers gathered on Tenterden Town station to watch the Rt Hon William Deedes break a bottle of wine over the front buffers of a happy little centenarian Stroudley Terrier Tank and declare the Kent and East Sussex Railway open. This marked the second spell of the standard gauge rural light railway's active life, for it was one of Colonel H. F. Stephens' light railways, first opened in March 1900. By the time he died in 1931, he had been involved with more than a dozen minor railways, designed to help country people to enjoy cheap transport, and without much concern for profit.

Originally the railway ran for 21½ miles from Headcorn on the main line from Tonbridge to Ashford across country in a southwesterly direction through Tenterden to Robertsbridge, on the Tonbridge to Hastings line. It kept its independence, although working closely with the Southern Railway, until the 1948 Nationalisation, but soon fell victim to British Railways' pruning measures and was closed by 1954. However, occasional hop-pickers' traffic

RIGHT No. 10, ex-LB&SCR 'Terrier' tank *Sutton*, on the Kent and East Sussex Railway.

BELOW No. 19, an ex-Norwegian State Railways 2–6–0 tender engine.

ran over its metals until July 1961, and then for ten years such tracks as were not pulled up rusted gently in the deep rural countryside.

But enthusiasts wanted to restore part of this attractive line and after several difficult years, which William Deedes, as M.P. for Ashford and a rail buff in his own right, helped to smooth, the Tenterden Railway Company was formed in 1971. The objective was to restore exactly 10 miles of line, from Tenterden south-westwards to Bodiam, famed for its castle.

A great deal of work had to be done, and still remains to be done, to reach Bodiam. At the time of writing, trains proceed from Tenterden to Wittersham Road station, about 4 miles away, and then return. Tenterden, attractive old market town (and former seaport when salt water once came in this far), needs to be the joining point for the railway. Once a week a 'wine and dine' special makes an evening return trip, taking its time as a social occasion merits. The K & ESR is one of the four 'Steam Lines South East' and is promoted by the South-East Tourist Board.

Highlight of the train ride is the climb up Tenterden Bank, more than a mile at 1 in 50, which is very steep for a standard gauge railway. The engine (or engines, for sometimes there is one on the end doing banking duties) works hard, puffing with extreme vigour and creating all those sights and sounds which lovers of steam travel miles to enjoy. The bank is on the way back from Wittersham; coasting downhill merely provides excellent views.

Rolvenden, first station out, is where the Preservation Company's workshops are located. Riders will see several stationary locomotives, some in a state of disrepair. The railway has some extremely interesting equipment, 21 engines at last count, one of them a 60 year old Norwegian import, a 2–6–0 retired from the Norwegian State Railways. There are two of the lovely little 0–6–0 'Terrier' tanks, Brighton engines over 100 years old. There are one or two diesels, and a former Great Western Railway express diesel railcar of pre-war days, one of the fast type intended for Birmingham–Cardiff express runs in the 1930s. In mid-September the K & ESR usually stages a 'spectacular' with up to a dozen steam engines coupled together tackling Tenterden Bank.

ABOVE NO. 23, *Holman F. Stephens* passing through the cornfields with an afternoon train for Wittersham Road.

Address Kent and East Sussex Railway, Tenterden Town Station, Tenterden, Kent TN30 6HE. Tel. Tenterden 2943

Enquiries to The Commercial Manager, at above address. Timetable available

Opening times Station open all year round, 10.00–17.00. Trains operate Easter to December (plus 1st January), weekends, Easter to October. Wednesdays, June–July, daily July–August

How to get there *By road* A28 to Tenterden. National Bus, No. 12 from BR stations at Headcorn, No. 400 from Ashford. National Express from Victoria. *By rail* to Ashford BR. Then bus

Facilities Car parking at Tenterden Town and Wittersham Rd, refreshments and souvenir shop

Special attractions 'Wealden Pullman' wine and dine service summer Saturday evenings, December 'Santa Specials'. Annual Steam and Country Fair

Discounts For groups.

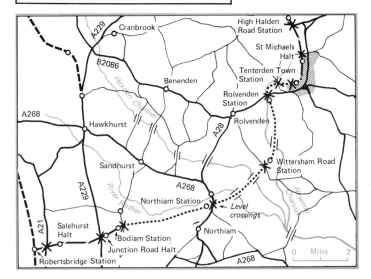

Bluebell Railway

On the 21st March, 1979, the 20th anniversary of Founder's Day for the Bluebell Railway, letters bearing special postmarks and a 15p Rail Letter Fee stamp, showing a Bluebell steam locomotive, were sent to many parts of the country.

The occasion marked two decades of successful work in providing a living standard gauge branch line museum of the late Victorian era. The Bluebell Preservation Society, formed in March 1959, was the first in Britain, indeed in the entire world, to tackle the problem of saving and operating a length of standard gauge passenger railway. It came eight years after the narrow gauge Talyllyn in Wales passed into the hands of willing, competent amateurs, and it meant hard work and machinery, for unlike tiny 2ft 6in (or smaller) gauge engines and rolling stock, standard gauge equipment cannot be manhandled.

The famous Adams radial tank, No. 488, hauls a rake of southern carriages through Lindfield Wood.

The Bluebell, as it is now, is 4½ miles of what was once a secondary line, built in 1882 between East Grinstead in Sussex and Lewes, the County Town. It runs from Horsted Keynes to Sheffield Park, through pastoral Sussex countryside and woodlands famed for their May displays of bluebells.

British Railways closed the line between East Grinstead and Lewes in 1958, although heavy local protests, in which Jimmy Edwards (the TV and film comedian) was involved as a Sussex resident, led to a temporary re-opening lasting nearly a year. When it finally closed, the Preservation Society managed to take over a limited section, despite having a mere £89 in the bank. The sum it had to find totalled £34,000, but there was an agreement to lease the 4½ miles of track for five years for £1,850 per annum. An further agreement in 1968 required a purchase price of £43,500 to include Horsted Keynes station, a once busy junction with four tracks. British Railways were paid £23,000 down with 20 quarterly payments of £1,000 to follow, a debt that was paid off well ahead of time. Sound annual profits have been recorded ever since, thanks to immense passenger support and excellent passenger loads.

Engines and rolling stock have been gathered from all over Britain and they are added to almost every year. The Bluebell now possesses about 15 steam locomotives and 25 coaches, by no means all vintage equipment.

There is a fine old Stroudley 'Terrier' tank, named *Fenchurch,* from the London, Brighton and South Coast Railway, dating from 1872, and a sister engine three years younger called *Stepney.* A 0–6–0 former South Eastern and Chatham tank engine dating from 1909 is named *Bluebell,* one of three sister engines owned by the line, which came from the steep Folkestone Harbour Branch. The collection also includes an express 4–6–0 from British

takes about 20 minutes each way. There is a branch line museum at Sheffield Park Station and one will soon be developed at Horsted Keynes. Horsted Keynes won second prize in the 1979 national contest to find the best kept station among Britain's preserved railways. Plans to extend the line northwards to East Grinstead have so far been unsuccessful.

Address Bluebell Railway, Sheffield Park Station, Nr Uckfield, East Sussex TN22 3QL. Tel. Newick 2370

Enquiries to Above address. Timetable available

Opening times Always open for limited viewing. Trains operate at weekends all year, weekdays in summer. See timetable for details

How to get there *By road* A275 to Sheffield Park, or unclassified lane off B2028 to Horsted Keynes. Bus Haywards Heath to Horsted Keynes (plus 20 minute walk). *By rail* to Haywards Heath BR (Awayday tickets available)

Facilities Car park, refreshments and souvenir and book shop

Special attractions Museum at Sheffield Park and historic collection of locomotives and rolling stock. Christmas specials

Discounts For groups of 15 or more. Children half-price

Railways, built in 1953, and a streamlined Bulleid Pacific from the Southern Railway dating from 1945. One particular engine draws visitors from all over the world and is included in railway publications from as far away as Japan, such is its fame and unique charm. The Adams 4–4–2 tank, one of three Radials which once worked the Lyme Regis branch in Dorset, is numbered 488 and was built in 1885. She lives with most of the others in the shed at Sheffield Park.

There is a set of four coaches from the old Metropolitan Railway built in 1898, also a collection of main line Southern Railway coaches from 1946 and three British Railways carriages from 1955. A splendid observation car from the London and North Western Railway (once used for viewing the Lake District) was built in 1913 and is used on many Bluebell trains, at an extra charge.

The original concept, to keep alive a former LB & SCR branch exactly as it was, has deviated a little, and engines in use are not all Southern or its constituents. One Great Western 'Dukedog', *Earl of Berkeley*, from 1938, sees service on the line, and from Scotland has come a former Caledonian Railway corridor composite carriage from 1920, a magnificent relic of the high point of rail coach building, but not appropriate to a late Victorian Sussex branch.

Trains may be joined at Sheffield Park or Horsted Keynes station and the ride

TOP LEFT Streamlined Bulleid Pacific 21C123 *Blackmore Vale* in the woods near Holywell with a train for Horsted Keynes.

CENTRE LEFT No. 592, ex-South Eastern and Chatham Railway, 0–6–0, with train at Sheffield Park Station.

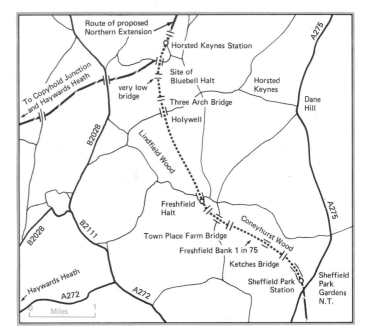

London Transport Museum

Science Museum

The London Transport Museum has recently opened in the old Flower Market in Covent Garden. It includes the collection that used to be on show at Syon Park, but this has been expanded considerably. Examples can be seen of trains, trams, trolley-buses and buses built over the past 150 years and owned by London Transport or its constituents. There are also uniforms, badges, signs and posters and displays of signalling equipment, sections through Underground tunnels, and other exhibits.

The Metropolitan Railway 4–4–0 tank (one of the original Underground condensing engines), the Metropolitan Railway electric locomotive *John Hampden*, and the City and South London 'padded cell' from 1890 (so called because it had no windows) early tube carriage are of particular interest.

For many decades, the Science Museum in South Kensington has been an early 'must' for young boys and girls. It still is but, with the profusion of railway museums all over Britain, it is no longer so important as the founding factor in giving a grounding in rail history. The static exhibits include the replica 1813 *Puffing Billy*, the original *Rocket* of 1829 and the original *Sanspareil* of 1829.

Most popular of the steam displays is the Great Western Railway *Caerphilly Castle*, first of the famous Castle Class from Swindon, built in 1923 and presented in 1961. There are eight full size steam engines to be seen, plus various models. The prototype English Electric Deltic diesel *Deltic*, built in 1955, is also on show, as is a typical London Underground coach from 1927.

BELOW LEFT London Transport Museum, Covent Garden.

RIGHT Dr Beeching (extreme left) handing over former GWR locomotive *Caerphilly Castle* to the Science Museum in 1961.

Address London Transport Museum, The Piazza, Covent Garden, London WC2. Tel. 01-379-6344

Enquiries to Above address

Opening times Daily, except 25th–26th December, 10.00–18.00.

How to get there Nearest Underground: Covent Garden

Facilities Refreshments and souvenir shop

Address The Science Museum, South Kensington, London SW7. Tel. 01-589 3456

Enquiries to The Information Dept at above address

Opening times Daily, afternoons only on Sundays. Closed on Good Friday, 24th–26th December, 1st January, 1st May. Admission free

How to get there *By road* to Exhibition Rd, South Kensington. *By rail* Nearest Underground: South Kensington

Facilities Refreshments, special canteen for schools

Volks Electric Railway

The centenary of electric traction on railways in 1979 brought an upsurge of interest in vintage trains hauled other than by steam. The first electric railway in Britain was built in Brighton by the Frenchman Magnus Volk. On 2ft gauge, it ran from the Aquarium to the Chain Pier, starting in August 1883. The carriages were mounted on stilts in later years, for operating over the breaking waves.

Volk died in 1937, at the age of 86. His railway, or a descendent of it, lives on, modernized in the years after the Second World War. It now runs on a gauge of 2ft 8½in and is operated by the County Borough of Brighton as a very frequent seaside pleasure train service, over 1½ miles of track between the original terminus at the Aquarium to Black Rock. There are three stations and two passing loops along the otherwise single (and fenced in) line. (Car parking can be a problem for visitors.)

Address Volks Electric Railway, 285 Madeira Drive, Brighton. Tel. Brighton 681061

Enquiries to Above address

Opening times Daily, March/April to October, 09.45–18.15 (later Bank Holidays and weekends). Trains every 6 minutes from each station.

How to get there *By road* to Palace Pier, Aquarium and *By rail* to Brighton BR

Discounts Negotiable for groups. Reduced rate for children

Volks Electric Railway

Romney, Hythe and Dymchurch Railway

ROMNEY HYTHE & DYMCHURCH
LIGHT RAILWAY

No 9 - Winston Churchill

Fee for conveyance of single post
Letter by Railway **10p**

ROMNEY HYTHE AND DYMCHURCH
LIGHT RAILWAY

No 8 - Hurricane 'The Royal Train'

Fee for conveyance of single post
Letter by Railway **15p**

My very first recollections of the miniature gauge main line running for 15 miles along the marshy Kent Coast to Dungeness are as a small boy visiting an uncle living at Hythe. We went as a party on the little train to New Romney to visit friends, treating the ride as a specific journey. With the doubtful exception of a wandering bus, there was no other way to go, and further along, to Dungeness, the little railway was the only method. Standard gauge trains of the Southern Railway came in from Lydd, and even then the denge marsh claimed victims among the Southern's heavier tank engines. But to go from Hythe to Lydd was a tremendous detour.

It was just the same in September, 1938. There were more buses but they did not extend to the marsh area. The 15 in gauge railway was still the vital transport link along the coast, in summer and in winter. Of course, it had its pleasures too, the miniature engines being steam and virtual replicas of big main line locomotives. During the War, Hythe was a restricted area. The Romney, Hythe and Dymchurch was on war service, armoured trains carrying guns along its tracks, but still it served the community with a basic

RH & DR letter stamps.

RIGHT *Dr. Syn* (No. 10) a 4–6–2 built in 1931 and modelled on North American types of the 1920s.

BELOW *Black Prince* (No. 11), built in 1937, hauling a train round Dungeness.

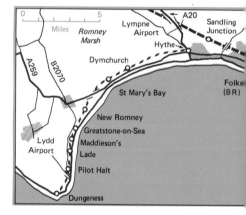

schedule for shoppers and schools.

Now the situation is completely changed, although the little railway survives intact, with its splendid engines just the same and heroically nostalgic. The owner and builder, Captain J. E. P. Howey, died in 1963, and the railway now operates as a consortium with pleasure travel its prime object. It is a member of 'Steam Lines South East'. More than 28 years have passed since genuine freight trains ran on its narrow metals, and a full winter schedule was last operated in 1948. A school contract signed recently means a term time run from Hythe to Dymchurch throughout the winter. It is largely due to Mr Bill McAlpine (owner of the *Flying Scotsman*) that the RH & DR survives, aided by Mr Brian Hollingsworth, and the support of association members and the issue of public shares.

This part of Kent is no longer wild and marshy, and even Dungeness can be penetrated by cars. Strengthening of the subsoil by the Army during the war made firm roads possible and weakened the position of the little railway.

But today the line flourishes in summer with tourist traffic. A ride provides a unique experience, for the RH & DR is a miniature main line, double track, with good signalling, and even healthy speeds such as 28 miles an hour (which feels like 75 m.p.h.). The locomotives look as though they are tearing along an express route such as the Great Northern to York, while a Canadian-style 'Pacific', *Winston Churchill*, or its sister engine *Doctor Syn* (named after the fictional smuggler of Dymchurch) recall the great days of the 1930s on the Montreal–Toronto CNR main line.

There are five LNER type 'Pacifics'

TOP *Typhoon* (No. 7), built in 1926, awaiting departure at Hythe Station.

CENTRE *Winston Churchill* (No. 9), built in 1931, outside the shed at New Romney.

LEFT *Hurricane* (No. 8) and *Winston Churchill* at New Romney.

31

dating from 1925–26, ordered by Captain Howey from Paxman's when he was having the line built, plus two rather bigger engines, 4–8–2s of British express type, also built by Paxman in 1926. The two Canadian-style engines came from the Yorkshire Engine Company in 1931, while a recent addition to motive power is a Krupp-built 'Pacific' of 1937. All but the Krupp have names, familiar to residents and holiday visitors to this part of Kent for more than half a century – *Green Goddess, Hurricane, Typhoon, Samson, Hercules, Northern Chief, Southern Maid.* There are one or two small diesel works engines.

No less than 48 good saloon coaches are in use, together with a dozen open bogies for fine weather, and a few other units. The seating is surprisingly good, two a side without cramping, and on the run to Dungeness, which takes an hour, no passengers suffer discomfort.

Hythe is the main station, but New Romney station has a museum and display and also the works and management headquarters. Trains can be joined at the stations along the route (Dymchurch, St Mary's Bay, New Romney, Maddieson's Camp, and Dungeness), where there are car parks and other facilities. Hythe has had no standard gauge railway since 1951; passengers alight at Sandling where there is an East Kent Bus.

Address Romney, Hythe and Dymchurch Railway, New Romney, Kent. Tel. New Romney 2353

Enquiries to The Manager, address as above. Timetable available

Opening times Daily, Easter to end September, also Saturdays and Sundays, March, October, November. See timetable for details

How to get there *By road* A20 from London to Ashford, then B2070 to New Romney, or to Newingreen, then A261 to Hythe. *By rail* to BR Folkestone Central. (Awayday tickets available). Bus routes 94 and 95 run direct to Hythe station

Facilities Car parks at all main stations, refreshments at Hythe, New Romney and Dungeness, souvenir shops at Hythe and New Romney Station

Special attractions Railway exhibition at New Romney station

Discounts For organized parties, booked in advance. Weekly runabout tickets also available. Children half-price

Sittingbourne and Kemsley Light Railway

In 1965, as part of an invited group with special interests, I travelled to Sittingbourne by Southern Region electric and soon came in contact with the industrial railway owned by Bowaters, the paper group. Little known at that time, the railway was a hive of activity, full of interesting little engines hard at work on the 2ft 6in gauge.

The locomotive stock amounted to 22 units, mostly tank engines, and very varied, including Mallet tanks (articulated). They hauled paper and other freight between Ridham Dock on the Swale Estuary and the mills at Sittingbourne. They also had passenger runs for employees to Kemsley and Ridham. Engines and rolling stock, in light green, were kept in superb condition, under the auspices of a few dedicated men. The Chief Mechanical Engineer had been there more than 30 years, long before 1948, when Bowaters took over the firm of Edward Lloyd Ltd, which constructed the lines in stages into the 1930s.

As senior men retired or died, the steam scene changed, diesels appeared, and road transport was substituted for the Ridham

Address Sittingbourne and Kemsley Light Railway Ltd, The Wall, Milton Regis, Sittingbourne, Kent, ME10 3HJ. Tel. Sittingbourne 24899

Enquiries to Mr W. E. Fuge, 48 Taverners Rd, Rainham, Gillingham, Kent ME8 9AN. Timetable available

Opening times April to October, Saturdays and Sundays; August only, Tuesdays, Wednesdays, Thursdays. 13.45–16.15 (17.15 Sundays)

How to get there *By road* to Light Railway Station in Milton Rd. *By rail* to Sittingbourne BR from Charing Cross and Victoria

Facilities Large free car park, refreshments and souvenir shop

Discounts For groups of 10 or more. Children half-price

run. In 1969 the railway was dead, but quick action on the part of the Locomotive Club of Great Britain and sympathetic co-operation by Bowaters revived part of it in 1970. A two mile section has survived, which today is open to the public.

The Sittingbourne and Kemsley Light Railway Ltd is a non-profit-making enterprise with about 500 members, formed at the end of 1971. It is now one of the four 'Steam Lines South East', and all trains are hauled by vintage locomotives. Some of the original Bowaters' stock has been sold to other railways where 2ft 6in gauge applies, but a number of engines are still on display at Kemsley Down, and others work the public train service.

The journey takes from 12 to 15 minutes each way and runs through level country towards the Swale, rural in places but with areas of waste land where former industrial plant and sidings were located. The passengers may ride in open or closed carriages, all vintage and atmospheric (in more ways than one).

Although the Light Railway Station can be reached by road, there is no road access whatever to Kemsley Down, and all train trips must be there and back, although passengers may alight and spend time between trains, viewing the static locomotive display, using the refreshment room and the picnic area.

Most of the narrow gauge engines have names. One of them, *Leader,* an 0–4–2 tank built by Kerr Stuart, dates from 1905, but the majority were constructed in the 1920s and 1930s, with the youngest, a Bagnall 0–6–2 tank *Superb* dating from 1940. There are two diesels for use with work trains.

All in all, the Sittingbourne and Kemsley is a happy little line, not as busy as it was in the days when it was working for Bowaters, but a fortunate survivor.

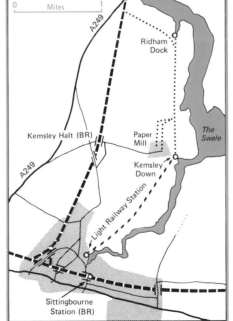

ABOVE Kerr Stuart 0–4–2 saddle tank *Premier* in a cutting north of Kemsley.

BOTTOM LEFT Bagnall 0–6–2 tank *Superb*, built in 1940.

AREA 2

THE SOUTH and WEST

WEST SOMERSET
RAILWAY

SOMERSET AND
DORSET RAILWAY
MUSEUM

BICTON WOODLAND
RAILWAY

FOREST RAILROAD
PARK, DOBWALLS

A30

DART VALLEY
RAILWAY

Plymouth

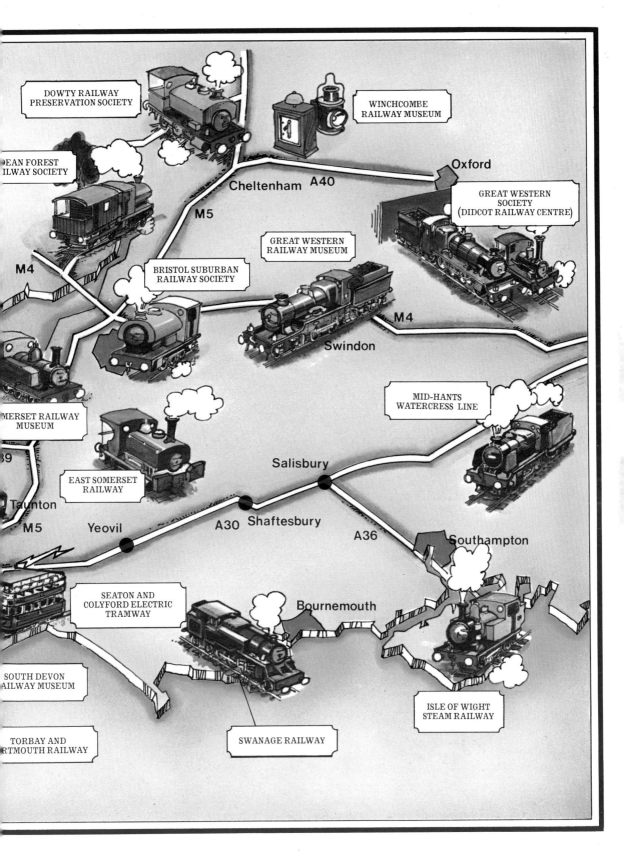

DOWTY RAILWAY
PRESERVATION SOCIETY

WINCHCOMBE
RAILWAY MUSEUM

DEAN FOREST
RAILWAY SOCIETY

Oxford

GREAT WESTERN
SOCIETY
(DIDCOT RAILWAY CENTRE)

Cheltenham   A40

M5

GREAT WESTERN
RAILWAY MUSEUM

M4

BRISTOL SUBURBAN
RAILWAY SOCIETY

M4

Swindon

MID-HANTS
WATERCRESS LINE

SOMERSET RAILWAY
MUSEUM

Salisbury

EAST SOMERSET
RAILWAY

39

Taunton

M5   Yeovil

A30   Shaftesbury

A36   Southampton

SEATON AND
COLYFORD ELECTRIC
TRAMWAY

Bournemouth

SOUTH DEVON
RAILWAY MUSEUM

ISLE OF WIGHT
STEAM RAILWAY

TORBAY AND
DARTMOUTH RAILWAY

SWANAGE RAILWAY

Great Western Railway Museum

Isle of Wight Steam Railway

Not to be confused with the Great Western Railway Society at Didcot, nor with several other societies of that name elsewhere, the *museum* is located in the heart of Swindon, the town created by the Great Western Railway Company during construction in the late 1830s. The setting is a former church with stained glass windows.

For a nominal entry fee, a number of static exhibits are revealed, some of them very famous in railway lore. There is the handsome 4–4–0 *City of Truro* which, in 1904 whilst hauling the 'Ocean Mail' from Plymouth to Bristol, tore down Whiteball Bank between Exeter and Taunton at a speed reported to be 102 miles an hour. Mr Charles Rous-Marten, Editor of the Railway Magazine was an observer on the footplate. She occupies a place of honour in the Museum close to the works where she was constructed in 1903.

Other engines include a big 4–6–0 (*Lode Star*), a typical GWR Pannier tank once so common all over that system, an elegant old Dean Goods 0–6–0 from 1887, and a replica of one of the very first GWR engines, the 2–2–2 broad gauge *North Star* of 1837. There are side chapels in the former church housing relics and paintings and posters, while highly polished nameplates from historic steam locomotives of Swindon parentage adorn the walls.

Address Great Western Railway Museum, Emlyn Square, Swindon, Wilts. Tel. Swindon 26161

Enquiries to The Curator, at above address

Opening times Monday to Saturday 10.00–17.00, Sundays 14.00–17.00. All year round, except Christmas, New Year's Day and Good Friday

How to get there *By road* M4, leaving by Exit 15. *By rail* to Swindon BR, 41 minutes from Paddington by high speed train

Facilities Parking nearby

Discounts Children half-price

Until 1966 the Isle of Wight was a living railway museum, with enchanting tank engines dating from the turn of the century and before, hauling elderly but handsome carriages on gentle journeys to sunny places. It was always a delight for people with a nostalgic frame of mind to alight from a ferry at Ryde Pier Head and see the waiting trains, one for Ventnor and one for Cowes, their green tank engines simmering at the head of a rake of carriages dating from before London area electrification schemes.

The little 0–4–4 tank engines all had names relevant to the island. They were sturdy and reliable, all 33 of them serving the Isle of Wight for more than 40 years, even after 30 and more years' service on London suburban duties.

In 1965 the Cowes line closed, and a year later the Ventnor line went, too, the end of steam on Wight being September 1966. The only surviving line, from Ryde Pier Head to Sandown, is now electrified and handled by former London Underground stock. It just does not, and cannot, give the same happy holiday feeling to new arrivals, although it carries vast numbers of people on summer Saturdays.

To keep the old feeling alive, the Isle of Wight Railway Company was formed immediately after closure, saving the 0–4–4 tank *Calbourne* and some rolling stock. This equipment is based at Haven Street station, 5 miles east of Ryde Esplanade. A section of the old line has been leased for 28 years to allow running for about 2½ miles to the site of the old station at Wootton (closed many years ago). The round trip takes about 35 minutes. A new station is being built near the former site, but tracks no longer run on to Newport.

A former LB&SCR 'Terrier' tank, built over a century ago as *Brighton* and now called *Newport*, shares duties with *Calbourne* and a couple of more modern industrial steam tank engines. Haven Street

also has a good collection of rolling stock with emphasis on the old Isle of Wight companies and the later Southern Railway. A Southern Pullman and Pullman kitchen car may be seen. More vintage equipment, including the Terrier tank from Hayling Island (a gift from Whitbread's) has recently been ferried to the island.

Address Isle of Wight Steam Railway, The Railway Station, Haven St, Nr Ryde, Isle of Wight PO33 4DS. Tel. Wootton Bridge 882204

Enquiries to Passenger agent, at above address. Timetable available

Opening times Easter weekend, May–September, Sundays; July–August Thursdays and Sundays, Bank Holidays, daily week preceding August Bank Holiday. 10.30–17.30

How to get there *By road* left off A3054 Ryde–Newport. Portsmouth–Ryde ferry. Southern Vectis routes 3 and 43. *By rail* to BR Ryde Esplanade

Facilities Free car park, souvenir shop and refreshments

Special attractions Museum. Unlimited travel on day of ticket issue

Discounts For groups

ABOVE On her 80th birthday, *Calbourne* (built 1891) hauls *Invincible* down the Ashey siding.

LEFT Hawthorn Leslie 0–4–0 saddle tank *Invincible* at Havenstreet.

BOTTOM Ex-LSWR 0–4–4 tank *Calbourne* at Wootton.

Great Western Society (Didcot Railway Centre)

While there are several Great Western Railway Societies flourishing in parts of Western England and Wales, the big one is at Didcot. In fact, Didcot has become synonymous with nuclear power plants and Great Western engines, the latter attracting by far the largest crowds. On major display days, as many as 25,000 people, ranging from the dedicated enthusiast to people who just enjoy seeing steam in action, gather at their famous engine shed close to the main line.

Access is through the British Rail station, where high speed trains call, and a sight for steam-eager eyes soon greets the visitor, for 22 former GWR engines are based there. On any Sunday from early April to late October the shed is open, but some days are declared major steaming occasions, when rides are given up and down a length of track. Steam days are held about 15 times each summer and on all Bank Holidays, with perhaps half a dozen of these events being major ones.

In addition to the steam stock, there are three diesel locomotives and two actual Great Western diesel railcars, plus thirty-two items of rolling stock, all of Great Western origin.

TOP RIGHT GWR travelling post office sorting van No. 814, built in 1940.

CENTRE RIGHT GWR Ocean Saloon No. 9112 *Queen Mary,* built in 1932.

BELOW Line up of GWR locomotives at Didcot Railway Centre.

Two Castle Class 4–6–0s, three Hall Class 4–6–0s, and one Manor 4–6–0 constitute the big passenger engine stock. There are several Prairie tanks, and a handful of popular pannier tanks, and an 0–4–2 tank once used extensively on GWR branches (until 1966 in fact). A big 2–8–0 freight engine of 28XX class built in 1940 is the most modern steam locomotive.

For many visitors, especially older ones to whom the Great Western was almost life itself, the display of rolling stock represents a top attraction. There is enough to furnish at least three genuine Great Western trains, and Didcot does so on those occasions when a steam special is going up to Birmingham Moor Street by way of Oxford and Banbury. There are 32 GWR coaches on hand, and a good deal of typical freight rolling stock. Three magnificent 'Ocean Saloons', dating from the 1932 Plymouth boat train, head the carriage collection, with an 1891 four-wheeled brake the oldest, while a Dean full brake of 1898 may be seen. A large number of solid GWR firsts and thirds from the peak days of the 1930s are there, too, and a 1951 first class sleeping car – the last type designed by the Great Western.

Address Great Western Society (Didcot Railway Centre), Didcot, Oxon

Enquiries to The Secretary, Great Western Society, Didcot, Oxon, OX11 7NJ. List of opening times available

Opening times April to October, Saturdays 12.00–17.00, Sundays and Bank Holidays 11.00–17.00

How to get there *By road* A34 Oxford to Newbury. *By rail* to Didcot BR

Facilities Car park, refreshment room and well-stocked shop

Special attractions Special steam days for schools in July

Discounts For families of 2 adults and 2 children. Children and OAPs half-price

---

CENTRE LEFT The signal box from Radstock, re-erected at Didcot Railway Centre.

CENTRE RIGHT GWR No. 1363 and No. 3738 in action at Didcot.

LEFT GWR 4–6–0 No. 7808 *Cookham Manor*, built at Swindon in 1938, with Ocean Saloon *Princess Elizabeth* behind the tender.

Mid-Hants 'Watercress' Line

The picturesque Hampshire town of Alresford (pronounced Arlesford) is the 'capital of Watercress'. All along the valley of the Itchen river, watercress is grown in profusion, and it used to be hauled by train on the Alton to Winchester secondary line of the Southern Railway.

British Rail tried to close this line in 1968 and finally succeeded in 1973 after vigorous local opposition. The Mid-Hampshire Railway Preservation Society was immediately formed, with ambitious plans to reopen it as both a working line and a steam railway for pleasure. Shares were issued by public subscription but insufficient funds came in for the purpose. After years of financial problems, what remains is the 3¼-mile stretch from Alresford to Ropley. On this, country-type steam trains are operated on Saturdays and Sundays to a locally published timetable. It is called the 'Watercress Line'.

There are still ambitious plans and new issues of shares, for the idea is to reopen the 7 miles of line between Ropley and Alton. British Rail is apparently willing to do all the relaying work for the Society for a charge of £50,000 per mile. But one

ABOVE Mid-Hants Railway Letter Stamp.

RIGHT Austerity 0–6–0 tank *Errol Lonsdale* at the water tower in Ropley Station.

wonders at all this – only six years ago the track was there, then BR took it up.

Meanwhile the 3¼ miles of active railway is very busy indeed, with enormous crowds turning up to ride the trains (often bigger than on the Bluebell Railway). The ride takes about 9 minutes from Alresford to Ropley, uphill all the way with gradients of 1 in 60 to 1 in 80 which makes the engine work with a strongly satisfying beat.

The official title of the line is the Winchester and Alton Railway Ltd, but although little hope remains of reaching Winchester, Alton could be achieved by 1983, giving a run of 10¼ miles and raising the Watercress Line to top status among working preserved railways, also linking it with BR's electric service at Alton. Today it is isolated and relies mostly upon car-

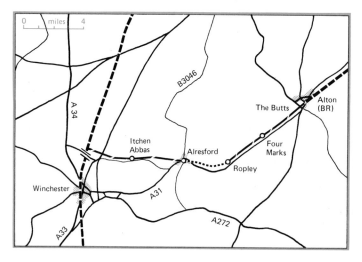

borne passengers, or a sparse country bus service.

The Mid-Hants 'Watercress' was a London & South Western secondary route, formerly operating trains from Alton to Southampton Docks. While there are some attempts to re-create an L S W R atmosphere, and also a Southern 'feel' of the 1930s, the enthusiast historian may be slightly disappointed in the trains often being run, with an ex-Longmoor Military Railway 0–6–0 saddle tank and five British Rail Mark 1 coaches.

The star of the line is restored West Country Bulleid Pacific *Bodmin*, which cost a fortune, and co-stars are three Moguls (2–6–0s), one an 'N' class (No. 31874) briefly named *Aznar Line* until that Spanish shipping Company abruptly dropped its Southampton ferry services, another a 'U', (No. 31806), the third, a BR standard from 1956, (No. 76017). The only surviving Urie 4–6–0, an S15 from 1920, is also on the line but not yet restored to working order. The powerful saddle tank *Errol Lonsdale* does much (some say too much) of the timetable work.

Headquarters are at Ropley Station, with a new shed and a collection of rolling stock including a genuine L S W R bogie coach. At present, trains operate frequently at weekends from Easter to October, but if the return to Alton could be achieved, all year working might be expected.

ABOVE Rebuilt 'West Country' Pacific No. 34016 approaches Ropley Station, a week before being named *Bodmin* for the second time.

LEFT No. 31874, recently re-named *Brian Fisk*, the only surviving SR 'N' class locomotive, built at Woolwich Arsenal in 1925.

Address Winchester and Alton Railway Ltd, Alresford Station, Alresford, Hants, SO24 9JG. Tel. Alresford 3810

Enquiries to The Information Dept, at above address. Timetable available

Opening times Saturdays, Sundays, Bank Holidays, last week in March to last week in October, 13.00–17.00 on Saturdays, 11.00–18.00 on Sundays, Bank Holidays

How to get there *By road* Alresford is on the A31 Guildford to Winchester. Ropley is slightly to the north of the A31. Alder Valley or Hants & Dorset buses. *By rail* to Alton or Winchester BR, then bus

Facilities Free car park at Alresford. Refreshment stalls and excellent souvenir shop at Ropley, and a shop, information office and Maunsell restaurant car serving light meals and snacks at Arlesford

Special attractions Locomotive shed at Ropley, entrance free to holders of valid rail tickets

Discounts For groups of 20 or more. Children and OAPs half-price

Winchcombe Railway Museum

Dean Forest Railway Society

This is a pleasant place in an indoor and outdoor garden setting in the village of Winchcombe, in Gloucestershire. It specializes in small exhibits with an emphasis on signalling equipment and lineside fixtures. Other historic relics may be seen, including photographs and paperwork, also lamps and bric-a-brac.

Address Winchcombe Railway Museum, 23 Gloucester St, Winchcombe, Glos. Tel. Winchcombe 602257

Enquiries to The Hon. Secretary, at above address

Opening times Easter, 1st May, Spring and Summer Bank Holiday Sundays and Mondays; Sundays, July and August; Daily 3rd–10th August

How to get there *By road* 8 miles from Cheltenham on A46 Stratford Road. *By rail* 'Castleways' bus from Cheltenham centre to Cheltenham Spa BR

Facilities Car park and souvenir shop

Discounts For groups of eight or more. Children, accompanied by adult, free

The Dean Forest Railway Society was formed in 1970 with the intention to acquire the freight-only branch line from Lydney (on the western side of the Severn) to Parkend in the Forest of Dean, a coal area. The intermediate station, Norchard, is the Society's base, which has been turned into a steam centre.

Until recently, the Society had equipment at Parkend but this has been vacated. The line is not yet available for running preserved steam trains although funds are available for leasing it if British Rail decide that the coal traffic is, indeed, extinct. Short yard steam trips are offered at times.

Unfortunately it must be said that the Forest of Dean conception has not made the progress expected of it. Instead of a happy little branch reopened to standard gauge steam, which looked to be the case in 1977, there is now one more parking area for veteran engines and rolling stock, with steam days about once a month and on Bank Holiday weekends. The steam centre is open every weekend in the afternoons for viewing static exhibits, which include

BELOW Peckett 0–4–0 saddle tank *Uskmouth* 1 in steam at the Norchard Steam Centre.

OPPOSITE Ex-GWR 2–6–2 tank No. 5541 in steam at Norchard with GWR auto-trailer No. 167.

South Devon Railway Museum

among the four steam engines, one diesel, and two coaches, a 0–6–0 Hunslet saddle tank from 1963. The rolling stock is mostly former Great Western, including an interesting auto-trailer from 1928. There are three signal boxes owned by members which would be erected if full permission was obtained to operate the line. Certain funds have been set up to acquire and restore a Great Western pannier tank and a 2–6–2 Prairie tank.

The museum has been moved from Parkend to Norchard.

Address Dean Forest Railway Society Ltd, Norchard Steam Centre, New Mills, Lydney, Glos. Tel. Lydney 3423

Enquiries to C. A. Bladon, Laurel Cottage, Northwood Green, Westbury-on-Severn, Glos.

Opening times April to October, Saturdays, Sundays and Bank Holidays, 11.00–18.00

How to get there *By road* ½ mile off A48 at Lydney along B4234. *By rail* to Lydney BR, then bus No. 40

Facilities Free car park, refreshments and souvenir shop

Special attractions Museum of small exhibits. 'Santa' steam day in December

Discounts By arrangement. Reduced rate for children

When Brunel engineered the South Devon Railway as a continuation of the Bristol and Exeter he decided on the atmospheric railway, fashionable and exciting in the early 1840s. The Atmospheric was a system by which air was pumped out of a length of pipe and a piston below the leading coach of a train moved along the pipe in the vacuum. The pipe was self-sealing behind the piston. Very successful for a brief period (when speeds of 80 miles per hour were obtained with silent trains, it soon failed as the pipe sealing wore out.

In South Devon, it worked for a while until all the snags allied to the vacuum method appeared, together with a worse one, when the big South Devon rats ate all the tallow used to reseal the tubes. The line was converted to regular steam operation after three years, but at its beginning trains had averaged 70 miles per hour between Exeter and Teignmouth (something they do not do even today) and one was reported as having hurtled through Dawlish Warren at 90 miles an hour! The South Devon Museum is located at Dawlish Warren station. There are very few relics of the old Atmospheric (although at Starcross up the line towards Exeter, the chimney of an original pumping station may be seen). But there are many small exhibits of interest, including locomotive name plates, old tickets, photographs, signs, number plates and railway bric-a-brac.

Address South Devon Railway Museum, Dawlish Warren Station, Dawlish, Devon

Enquiries to Above address

Opening times Daily, April to end September, 11.00–17.00

How to get there *By road* Off A379 to Teignmouth. *By train* to Dawlish Warren BR

Discounts Children half-price

Headlamp from the Dean Forest Railway Society Collection.

East Somerset Railway

Mr David Shepherd is well-known for his magnificent paintings of steam locomotives and elephants. In railway circles he is lauded for his successful work as Chairman of the 'Return to Steam' movement, which brought back locomotives in good condition to certain sections of line owned by British Railways.

He has two big engines of his own, now kept in a permanent home at Cranmore, East Somerset. They were previously located at various centres, including the now defunct Longmoor Military Railway in Hampshire. Cranmore was a station on the old Cheddar Valley line of the Great Western, closed in 1963 apart from a section, used for stone quarries, which reached to Cranmore. Mr Shepherd and his followers were responsible for taking over the ½-mile from the quarries to Cranmore station, building a modern engine shed (in period style), restoring Cranmore station to its former state, and housing his engines. The East Somerset Railway became a living entity by the mid-1970s.

Visitors will see the huge 2–10–0 9F class engine *Black Prince* (built as recently as 1959), a modern 4–6–0 of post-war

design now named *The Green Knight,* and a former Southern Railway Schools 4–4–0, No. 928 *Stowe,* which used to be at Lord Montagu's car museum at Beaulieu in Hampshire and is still jointly owned by Lord Montagu. There is also a small Dubs 0–4–0.

Address East Somerset Railway, Cranmore Railway Station, Cranmore, Nr Shepton Mallet, Somerset BA4 4QP. Tel. Cranmore 417

Enquiries to Above address. Timetable available

Opening times April to October, 9.00–17.30 daily, November to March, Saturday and Sunday only, 9.00–16.00. Steam on Sundays, Bank Holidays and Special Events

How to get there *By road* off A361 Shepton Mallet to Frome. *By rail* to Frome BR, then bus

Facilities Large free car park, refreshments and souvenir shop

Special attractions Signal Box Art Gallery with wide selection of David Shepherd's railway prints. Full-size replica of Victorian-style steam depot

Discounts For groups. Children and OAPs half-price

BOTTOM RIGHT David Shepherd's huge 2–10–0 9F class engine, *Black Prince,* with the Austerity engine No. 68005.

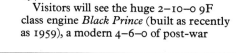

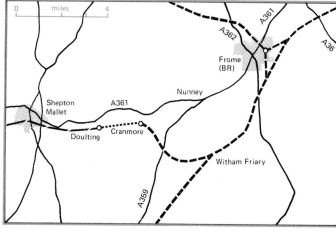

Somerset and Dorset Railway Museum

Swanage Railway

Situated at Washford station, $5\frac{3}{4}$ miles from Minehead on the West Somerset Railway (see page 48), this Museum Trust is still constructing its base. It aims to preserve what little remains of the famous and well-liked Joint Railway with its blue engines which served – albeit rather slowly and in vintage style – the rural communities of Dorset and Somerset and linked by main line the resort of Bournemouth and the spa of Bath.

The public is admitted at own risk while construction continues, but the site is open at weekends and on Bank Holidays. Engines are steamed from time to time with short steam rides given in the station area. Locomotives and rolling stock have been moved to Washford from a former depot at Radstock, and are mostly industrial tank engines and National Coal Board wagons, but the main exhibit is a genuine 2–8–0 from the Somerset and Dorset (that railway's, No. 88), built in 1925 and repainted blue (although it may never have worked in that colour). It is at present undergoing extensive repairs.

In the station buildings a museum of S & D J R relics has been established. Revived interest in the old Joint Line all over the two counties is helped by an artist, Mrs Moira Hawkes of Catcott (near the site of the S & D's Edington Junction) who has painted several fine oils of early steam scenes.

When the $11\frac{1}{2}$-mile branch of Southern Region from Wareham Junction to Swanage was cut off in 1972, a group of enthusiasts formed the Swanage Railway Company Ltd, with intent to revive the line through its scenic Dorset hills.

Since then a great deal of hard work has been done, enlisting aid and sponsors and in discussions with the County Council, but despite a compromise proposal to relay the $6\frac{1}{2}$-mile line to Corfe Castle, the intermediate station, all there is to show for eight year's effort is a totally preserved railway station and three engines.

Swanage station, right in the middle of the attractive resort, is full of railwayana, and has a 2–6–4 British Rail standard tank of the type which hauled the branch trains in the last ten years or so of service. There is also a Barclay 0–4–0 tank *Richard Trevithick*. A small works diesel waits hopefully for some track work to do.

Periodically, there is a blaze of hope, and steamings held in August 1979 revived expectations. For visitors to Swanage and the Purbeck Peninsula, a look at the station and its relics is worthwhile, and steam operations should grow in the next few years.

Barclay 0–4–0 tank *Richard Trevithick* leaves Swanage with the Pines Express on the first day of operation.

Address Somerset and Dorset Railway Museum, Museum Trust, Washford Station, Nr Watchet, Somerset

Enquiries to Above address

Opening times Weekends and Bank Holidays

How to get there *By road* A39 Bridgwater to Barnstaple. *By rail* to Taunton BR and West Somerset train service from Minehead

Facilities Limited car parking, souvenir shop, adjacent Washford Hotel provides lunches and teas

---

Address Swanage Railway Co Ltd, Swanage Station, Swanage, Dorset. Tel. Swanage 2506 or Fleet 24469

Enquiries to The Secretary, Swanage Railway Co Ltd, The Station House, Dorset *or* The Publicity Officer, 28 Sycamore Crescent, Church Crookham, Aldershot, Hants GU13 0NN

Opening times March to October, mainly weekends

How to get there *By road* A351 to Swanage, access through station car park. *By rail* to Wareham BR, then bus

Facilities Car park, refreshments and souvenir shop

Seaton and Colyford Electric Tramway

Visitors to the South Devon Coast, east of the estuary of the Exe, are sometimes very surprised to see small open-top tramcars moving along quite fast through the pastures. They offer a pleasant little ride between Seaton and Colyton, about $2\frac{1}{2}$ miles, over the track-bed of the former Seaton Junction to Seaton (and Budleigh Salterton) branch of the Southern Region.

Laid to a gauge of 2ft 9in, the tramcars, seven of them all looking like the full size open-top vehicles so familiar in British cities in the 1920s and 1930s, came from Eastbourne. They were not part of that resort's official public transport, but ran a pleasure service along the eastern beach areas of Eastbourne in the region known as the Crumbles.

There is talk of further extensions down in South Devon (the line has already in-creased its length by $\frac{3}{4}$ mile since the transfer about a decade ago).

Address Seaton and Colyford Electric Tramway, Harbour Rd, Seaton, Devon

Enquiries to The General Manager, at above address

How to get there *By road* B3161 to Colyton, B3172 to Seaton; off A3052 Lyme Regis to Sidmouth. *By rail* to Exeter BR and bus, or Exmouth and No. 40 bus

Opening times Late May to end September, limited service during Easter Week. Half-hourly service at peak periods

Facilities Car park at both ends of the run, and souvenir shop

---

CENTRE AND BOTTOM RIGHT The narrow gauge open top tramcars operating along the seafront in Eastbourne in the mid-1950s.

LEFT The same tramcars now work between Seaton and Colyton in Devon.

Bicton Woodland Railway

The Bicton, a very narrow gauge line of 1 ft 6 in gauge, built in 1963, runs on track within the famous Bicton Gardens near Budleigh Salterton in Devon. These gardens at East Budleigh are reckoned among the most attractive in the West Country, with a lake and a pinetum rather than an arboretum. Owners are the Rolle Estate, East Budleigh.

The railway is a steam attraction quite close to the Seaton and Colyford light tramway, and a ride on it is offered as an extra amenity to those visiting the Gardens. Two small steam engines and two diesels handle the traffic, the Avonside 0–4–0 tank from 1961 and a 'Mallet' 0–4–4–0 Hunslet from 1954 being of special interest. The rolling stock used is open bogies on fine days and covered bogies during inclement weather.

It is possible that further extensions may be made to the Countryside Museum, where steam engines and early agricultural equipment are displayed.

Address Bicton Woodland Railway, Bicton Gardens, Budleigh Salterton, Devon. Tel. Colaton Raleigh 68465

Enquiries to Rolle Estate Office, East Budleigh, Devon

Opening times Gardens open, daily Easter to end October, 10.00–18.00. Trains daily in summer

How to get there *By road* A376 Budleigh Salterton to Newton Poppleford. *By rail* to Exmouth BR, then No. 334 bus

Facilities Free car park, gift shop and refreshment room

Discounts For groups. Children reduced

BOTTOM LEFT Avonside 0–4–0 tank *Woolwich*, built in 1916, on Bicton Woodland Railway.

BELOW The open rolling stock behind a diesel.

West Somerset Railway

TOP Water tower at Minehead.

CENTRE Stogumber station building.

The seaside resort of Minehead, nestling below the brooding heights of Exmoor and facing into the wide Bristol Channel, was a Great Western terminus for over a century. On summer Saturdays, heavy express trains ran through from Paddington and even on winter weekdays there was a good service to Taunton with frequent fast connecting trains to London.

Eight years after the Beeching Report was published and six years after the hated Axe was falling on branch and secondary lines all over the land, the 23 miles from Norton Fitzwarren, on the former Great Western main line between Taunton and Exeter to Minehead, were closed to all traffic. How that latter day blow fell is still not clear, but the tracks were left intact and almost as soon as British Railways traffic stopped, a West Somerset Railway Company was formed. By March 1972, an agreement for the purchase price of the whole line had been concluded with BR, and then the Somerset County Council became interested, agreeing to purchase the line and to lease it back to the West Somerset Railway.

Unhappily, trains are still not running over the full and effective length of the branch. Its full potential has not been, and cannot be, reached because Taunton is the main point of connection. As things stand, with trains only running between Minehead and Bishop's Lydeard ($19\frac{3}{4}$ miles), the West Somerset is not quite impacting. By now it should be the longest preserved line in the country, with an effective winter service earning revenue through providing services such as school trains and shoppers' trips. There has been opposition from local landowners, from changed attitudes on the County Council, from the National Union of Railwaymen (who have not objected to such lines elsewhere in the country) and from Western Region itself, who oppose WSR trains junctioning and running parallel into Taunton. Currently there is bus connection from Bishop's

Lydeard to Taunton (5 miles) to link with diesel trains which do, however, run all year.

However, the 20 miles of pleasure line are indeed a pleasure, and some residents of places such as Watchet, Williton, Stogumber and Bishop's Lydeard can use the trains to visit Minehead. Steam services run usually only from Minehead to Blue Anchor on weekdays, a 13 minute ride, but on Sundays they go through to Williton, $9\frac{3}{4}$ miles in 41 minutes, and on Saturdays they run the $19\frac{3}{4}$ miles to Bishop's Lydeard in an hour.

Diesels operate the rest of the services, which in summer are fairly frequent between early May and the beginning of October. Timetables are issued and are also published in the ABC, and will be found a trifle complicated, with numerous annotations such as 'Tuesdays and Thursdays only'. This winter saw a daily service with diesels to Bishop's Lydeard, except for Sundays. The West Somerset is nearing its goal but the last 5 miles may prove very difficult.

The West Somerset has, like several other preserved lines, had a good financial and publicity boost by being chosen for both series of the *Flockton Flyer* made by Southern Television. The West Somerset Steam Railway Trust Ltd also supports the Company and provides engines and rolling stock. At Washford Station the Somerset and Dorset Museum (see page 45) is a further attraction with relevant engines and rolling stock.

Pride of the West Somerset are former Great Western 'Prairie' tanks (2-6-2) which actually worked the branch for some 35 to 40 years. Three of them are currently stored at Bishop's Lydeard, a station just open to traffic. Most steam trains are hauled by former industrial tanks, modern 0-6-0's from Bagnall's, or by the 0-6-0 pannier tank from the GWR, which starred in the *Flockton Flyer*. There is a powerful Hymek Diesel

Somerset Railway Museum

built in 1961, and a diesel multiple unit, plus a couple of diesel shunters.

There are 14 passenger coaches on the line, both period and modern, not including the diesel multiple unit. Several brake vans and an unusually large number of wagons give the railway a professional atmosphere with the appearance of a potential freight service.

Minehead is headquarters of the line, with car parking (often full on summer Saturdays), a good café and souvenir shop. Washford (see page 45) and Bishop's Lydeard are worth seeing for the equipment on view there.

Within the outer limits of Bristol Suburban is Bleadon and Uphill Station, actually close to Weston-super-Mare on the Bristol to Bridgwater and Taunton main line. The station has long since been closed although trains pass through it at speed. The station is privately owned and called 'Somerset Railway Museum'. In the building are displays of relics, while outside rest a few industrial engines including a Sentinel from 1947 and a BR railbus from 1958. Parking is easy in the station yard; visitors are not numerous and confined largely to dedicated enthusiasts.

Address West Somerset Railway, The Station, Minehead, Somerset. Tel. Minehead 4996

Enquiries to Above address. Timetable available

Opening times Daily diesel service all year. Steam in summer

How to get there *By road* A39 Bridgwater to Barnstaple. *By rail* to Taunton BR

Facilities Car park and café at Minehead, souvenir and book shops at Minehead and Blue Anchor Museum

Discounts for families, groups, OAPs

Address Somerset Railway Museum, Bleadon and Uphill Station, Nr Weston-Super-Mare, Avon

Enquiries to Above address

Opening times On request

How to get there *By road* A370 Weston-Super-Mare to Highbridge. *By rail* to Weston-Super-Mare BR

Facilities Car park

The West Somerset Railway's ex-GWR 0–6–0 pannier tank No. 6412 starred in Southern TV's *The Flockton Flyer*.

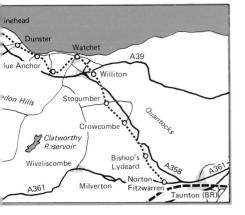

Dowty Railway Preservation Society

This large depot and collection of engines and rolling stock at Ashchurch near Tewkesbury in Gloucestershire provides a home for major engines as well as preserving some interesting types. It was formed by members of the Dowty Industries Sports and Social Society in 1962, and has gone from strength to strength, but is not a railway as such, offering visitors just an occasional ride on siding track.

The Heart of England Tourist Board lists it as one of the major visitor attractions of Gloucestershire in the industrial scene, praising the Society for the restoration of Avonside 0–4–0 tank *Cadbury Bournville No.* 1 built in 1925 and the Great Western Railway special saloon No. 9044 built in 1881 and once used in a Royal train.

Most big engines have moved on to other sites since the 'Return to Steam' became possible, but Dowty gave them a home when they most needed it. There is a large 0–6–0 Q class of the former Southern Railway on the site, as well as a few industrial tank engines, nine diesels of various kinds, and seven coaches.

A 2 ft gauge collection is also stored at Ashchurch, including a Jung 0–4–0 well tank from 1906 (named *Justine*). A large collection of signalling, station, and lineside equipment is well worth inspecting.

The Dowty Shed complex is open for static displays and occasional steamings. All volunteer work is concentrated upon restoration and maintenance, with no intention of obtaining a length of line for running trains beyond the depot.

Towards the end of 1980, the Dowty collection will be moving a short distance, due to major road developments.

Address Dowty Railway Preservation Society, Northway Lane, Ashchurch, Nr Tewkesbury, Glos.

Enquiries to Above address. Timetable available

Opening times Every weekend, 14.00–16.00 for static display. See local press for steam days

How to get there *By road* A438 from Tewkesbury, left at Northway Lane ¼ mile after crossing M5 (exit 9). *By rail* BR Cheltenham Lansdown

Facilities Free car park and good souvenir shop

BOTTOM LEFT Avonside 0–4–0 tank *Cadbury Bournville No.* 1.

RIGHT This Midland Railway California Crossing signal box is a recent arrival at Ashchurch and now controls the narrow gauge station and yard.

Bristol Suburban Railway Society

Based at the former Midland Railway station of Bitton, $8\frac{1}{2}$ miles from Bristol on the one-time suburban line between Bristol and Bath via Mangotsfield, the Bristol Suburban Railway Society was formed with the laudable intention of re-opening this route, plus a branch to Yate. As with so many of these schemes, being excellent ideas but short of capital and lacking the support of the former owners, it has not proceeded very far.

The suburban population in the area is very large, and if sufficient backing in the new climate can be obtained, this project should succeed, being the first of its kind to offer a genuine suburban steam service. Meanwhile, the Society has just a mile of track running to the north of Bitton.

Their major preserved locomotive is a Stanier Black Five 4–6–0, No. 45379, built in 1937. There are three industrial engines, each from a different Bristol-based engineering works (Peckett, Avonside, and Fox Walker). A yard diesel shunter, an ex-LMS brake van and two covered vans are also owned.

The centre is opened at various times throughout the year for steamings and for short brake van rides especially on Bank Holidays.

Address Bristol Suburban Railway Society, Bitton Railway Centre, Bitton, Bristol

Enquiries to Mr E. H. Amos, 32 Milford Ave, Wick, Bristol. Timetable available

Opening times Every weekend. Steam days in March, April, May, June, July, September, October, December

How to get there *By road* A431, Bristol to Bath road. Bus No. 332 from Bristol. *By rail* to BR Keynsham or Bath Spa

Facilities Large car park, refreshments and souvenir shop

Discounts For groups. Children, one-third discount

Special attractions Schools' week in July

ABOVE Ex-LMS Stanier Class Five standing at Bitton.

LEFT Avonside 0–6–0 saddle tank *Edwin Hulse* awaiting the 'all clear' during an open day at Bitton.

Dart Valley Railway

The Dart Valley, one of the most successful preserved systems in Britain, is the only one to have two divisions although, sadly, they are not connected by their own tracks. The first section was the revival of the delightful former Great Western branch line which ran beside the upper reaches of the Dart from Totnes to Ashburton. Then came the virtual take-over of a main line, the section of the Newton Abbot to Kingswear (Dartmouth) abandoned by British Rail between Paignton and Kingswear.

Both lines offer a pleasant steam train ride through some of the most enchanting

RIGHT GWR 4–6–0
No. 4920 *Dumbleton Hall*,
built in 1929.

BELOW GWR Super
Saloon *King George*, built
in 1932.

scenery of South Devon, and are naturally highly popular with holidaymakers. At one stage the Torbay section to Kingswear ran all year round, the main winter business being the conveyance of schoolchildren.

The Totnes and Ashburton was closed to all traffic by British Rail in 1962 and efforts to revive it as a complete branch have been unsuccessful due to road schemes affecting the final mile or so beyond Buckfastleigh. However, the Dart Valley Light Railway Company, formed by enthusiasts with public subscriptions to aid them, restored the 7 miles between a point near to the main line station at Totnes and Buckfastleigh station.

Buckfastleigh, close to the famous Abbey where tonic wines are produced, is headquarters of the section where locomotives and rolling stock are stored and maintained. At the Totnes end there is as yet no access to the British Rail station, and in fact the junction was cut out abruptly in the days before BR became more co-operative towards preserved lines. A new Dart Valley station is under construction less than $\frac{1}{4}$ mile from the BR station, but meanwhile passengers join

trains either at Buckfastleigh or the intermediate station of Staverton Bridge (where rakes of rolling stock are sometimes stored on open sidings).

It is usual for passengers to make the round trip from Buckfastleigh. The atmosphere is purely Great Western Railway, with the right kind of engine and carriages. Sometimes one of the beautiful former Ocean Liner Saloons is attached to a train, and used for a private party. The 'super-saloon' named *King George* was built by the GWR in 1932 for its Plymouth boat specials, and is now the property of the Dart Valley Railway Association.

The better direction is the climb up the Dart Valley, with the river almost always in sight, towards the edge of Dartmoor, and the engine working quite hard. But whichever way one rides, the scenery is delectably rural and the feeling one gets is being transported back in time to happy Devon branchlines. Not far short of 200,000 passengers enjoy this 14-mile round trip in a full season.

There is a great deal of interesting equipment on the Dart Valley section. Pride of the line is a big Great Western engine, *Dumbleton Hall*, a 4–6–0 built in 1929. The 14 other steam engines are all tanks, including an interesting 2–8–0 called *Thunderer*, and a fairly modern, powerful British Railways 2–6–4 tank from 1953. Two very charming 0–4–2 tanks from Great Western days of the 14XX class are favourites, because they were the types which hauled most traffic over the line in Great Western and immediate post-GWR days (as they did on

many West Country and West Midlands branch lines).

The line possesses one Drewry diesel, no less than ten Wickham petrol rail trolleys, and five former GWR auto-trailers. The rolling stock is GWR with only the odd exception (a Gresley buffet car from the London and North Eastern Railway and an ex-LMSR truck). The stock ranges from the super-saloon and standard open carriages to a banana van. Some 15 carriages can be used on holiday passenger trains, which are daily in summer and take 55 minutes round-trip. Services are boosted on steam gala weekends.

Approaching a level crossing on the Dart Valley Railway.

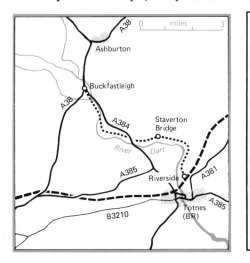

Torbay and Dartmouth Railway

The Torbay and Dartmouth Railway, operated by the Dart Valley Railway Company, starts its journey from a new side-extension at Paignton main line station, effecting a good connection with British Rail trains arriving from Paddington, which now terminate there. The resort's bus station is only a stone's throw away.

The seven miles of track to Kingswear were abandoned by British Rail at the end of 1972's summer season, ten years after trains last ran on the Totnes and Ashbur-ton branch. The Dart Valley Light Railway Company Ltd immediately bought the tracks to Kingswear, getting for their money a fine stretch of railway including a tunnel $\frac{1}{4}$ mile long and a steep bank up 1 in 60, a severe test of engine power with a heavy train. There is also the restored structure of a once-busy junction, Churston (where the 2-mile Brixham branch went off), and some high viaducts. A former halt also survived, now Goodrington Sands.

RIGHT GWR 2–8–0 tank No. 5239 *Thunderer* as it passes through Goodrington BR yard.

BELOW GWR No. 7827 4–6–0 *Lydham Manor* at Paignton Station yard.

The journey time, with stops at both intermediate stations, is 35 minutes each way. Passengers may alight at the stations and cross on the ferry from Kingswear to Dartmouth. There is an amusing note in the Torbay timetable stating that the 14.15 train to Kingswear – 'will be held to connect with the 10.55 from Paddington if that train is running to time'.

Members of the Dart Valley Railway Association, hard-working volunteers, help with the running of this line as they do with the Totnes to Ashburton. They also own some of the equipment. In return for their work they get a certain number of free journeys per annum on both lines.

The trip to Kingswear is extremely attractive, running close to the sea along Torbay with views to Bury Head, and then striking inland to climb the lovely South Devon hills and descend into the lower Dart valley, with a panorama of Dartmouth and the Royal Naval College on the opposite shore. The final $1\frac{1}{2}$ miles run beside the river into the old Great Western terminus, once linked by a GWR ferry to a station on the western bank which had no railway tracks. Today's passengers must walk a bit to the regular vehicle chain ferry.

Some thought has been given over the years to the possible resurrection of the 2 miles of branch line to Brixham, but so much building has taken place on and near its course since it was taken up (many years before closure of the Kingswear line) that relaying it would probably prove too costly. If it were possible, however, it would give the Dart Valley three sections

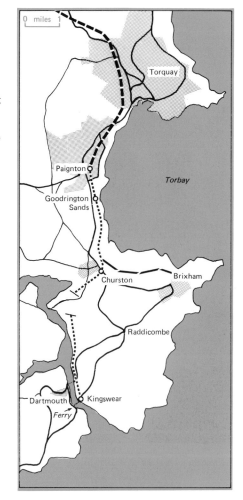

Pullman Observation Car
Devon Belle.

and create the first real branch off a main line on any preserved system.

Such are the attractions to both the holidaymaking public and a hard core of railway enthusiasts that visiting engines of considerable fame are found on the Torbay Railway from time to time. The legendary *Flying Scotsman* has worked many a train to Kingswear. Transfer of engines and rolling stock, not only from some distant part of England but also from the Totnes and Ashburton, must either be by courtesy of British Rail, who of course own the tracks from Paignton to Torquay and Newton Abbott, and to Totnes, or by low-loader road vehicle.

In normal circumstances, there are three active steam engines and two diesels on the Torbay Railway. One of the 'Western' type diesel-hydraulic locomotives, retired by British Rail after 15 years service at the end of 1977, runs some Torbay trains. This particular type of Swindon-built diesel is held in high regard by a large number of rail enthusiasts, who confer upon 'Westerns' virtually the status of honorary steam engines.

Although not so strictly 'Great Western' as its upper Dart division, the Torbay line predominantly reflects that much loved Company. Pride of its power stock is the 4–6–0 *Lydham Manor*, actually built by BR to GWR design at Swindon in 1950. There is also a Prairie tank (2–6–2 from 1927), called *Warrior*. One of the super-saloons lives at Paignton, and another magnificent carriage, the observation Pullman from *Devon Belle*, is a set piece. There are several modern open-type British Rail coaches, nine 'seconds' and two 'firsts'.

RIGHT *Lydham Manor* crosses Hookhills viaduct near Churston with the 'Torbay Express'.

BELOW GWR 2–6–2 tank No. 4588 *Warrior* steams away from Churston.

Address Torbay and Dartmouth Railway, Queens Park Station, Paignton, Devon. Tel. Paignton 555872

Enquiries to General Office, at above address. Timetable available

Opening times Easter, daily late May to end September

How to get there *By road* A379 to Paignton. *By rail* to Paignton BR

Facilities Car park, refreshments and souvenir shop

Special attractions Paignton GWR 'EM' gauge model railway, Royal Dart buffet and bar at Kingswear

Discounts For groups of over 20. Reduced rate for children

Forest Railroad Park, Dobwalls

In the unlikely surroundings of Cornish granite and woodlands near Dobwalls, fairly close to the British Rail station of Liskeard, the atmosphere and rail operation of Wyoming a quarter of a century ago have been reproduced. Built as recently as 1970, this miniature railway is only 7¼in gauge, but its passenger-hauling models are indeed gigantic.

There is a reproduction of a Union Pacific 'Big Boy', a class of articulated 4–8–8–4 Mallet which was the biggest steam engine in the world when introduced in 1941. The class remained in service, working over the steep gradients nearly 1½ miles above sea level in the Cheyenne-Laramie region of Wyoming until 1959. Another Union Pacific type engine, a 4–8–4, is called *Queen of Wyoming*, built in 1974, plus a Denver and Rio Grande model, in this case a 2–8–2 built in 1972 (named *General Palmer*). A works diesel also has Western America outlines.

More than a mile of 7¼in gauge track is now in use, with a remarkable reconstruction of the famous 'Sherman Hill' where the real Union Pacific crosses the high plain on the Overland Trail 7,700ft above sea level. The Cornish one is on the same scale, causing the model engines to climb a 1 in 66 gradient. The whole layout of the Forest Railway is severe and scenic,

claimed to be 'the most arduous of any miniature gauge line in the country'. The track is mainly single but with sections of double to allow realistic passing, while multiple aspect colour light signals are fitted.

The railway is an ideal visitor attraction for families touring this part of Cornwall, especially Looe, and for anyone with an interest in Rocky Mountain 'railroading' it is a must. Fair weather is desirable as the coaches are open bench type.

Address Forest Railroad Park, Dobwalls, Cornwall. Tel. Dobwalls 20325

Enquiries to Mrs G. Arnold, at above address. Timetable available

Opening times Easter, 10 days beginning Good Friday, daily, 10.30–17.30. Until 1st May, Sundays and Wednesdays only, 12.00–17.30. 1st May to 5th October, daily 10.30–17.30

How to get there *By road* to Dobwalls ½ mile north of A38. *By rail* to Liskeard BR, about 3 miles away

Facilities Large car park, picnic areas, children's play areas, refreshments, and souvenir shop

Special attractions Large indoor model railway exhibition

Discounts For groups

A model of the world's largest steam locomotive – Union Pacific Big Boy *William Jeffers* – on the Sherman Hill Route in Forest Railroad Park.

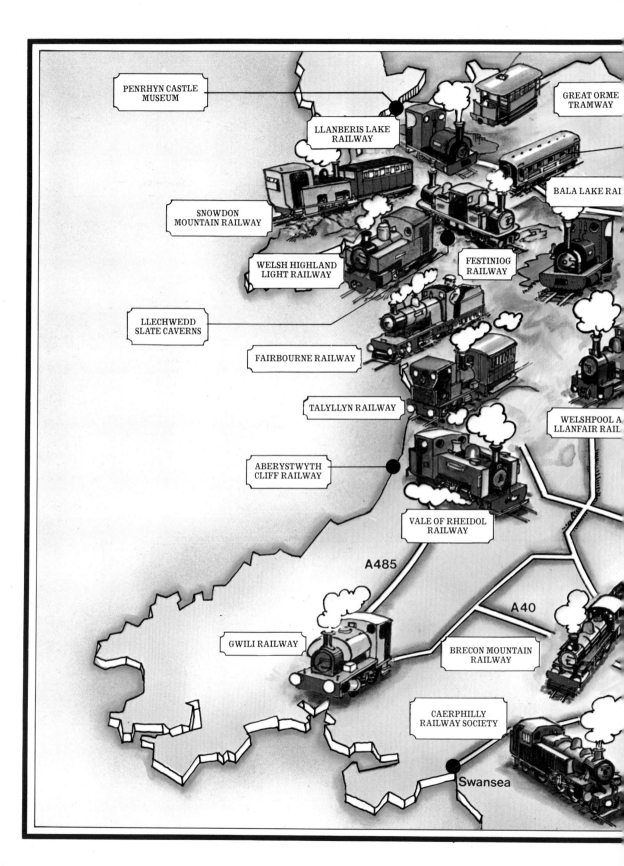

PENRHYN CASTLE
MUSEUM

LLANBERIS LAKE
RAILWAY

GREAT ORME
TRAMWAY

BALA LAKE RAI

SNOWDON
MOUNTAIN RAILWAY

WELSH HIGHLAND
LIGHT RAILWAY

FESTINIOG
RAILWAY

LLECHWEDD
SLATE CAVERNS

FAIRBOURNE RAILWAY

TALYLLYN RAILWAY

WELSHPOOL A
LLANFAIR RAIL

ABERYSTWYTH
CLIFF RAILWAY

VALE OF RHEIDOL
RAILWAY

A485

A40

GWILI RAILWAY

BRECON MOUNTAIN
RAILWAY

CAERPHILLY
RAILWAY SOCIETY

Swansea

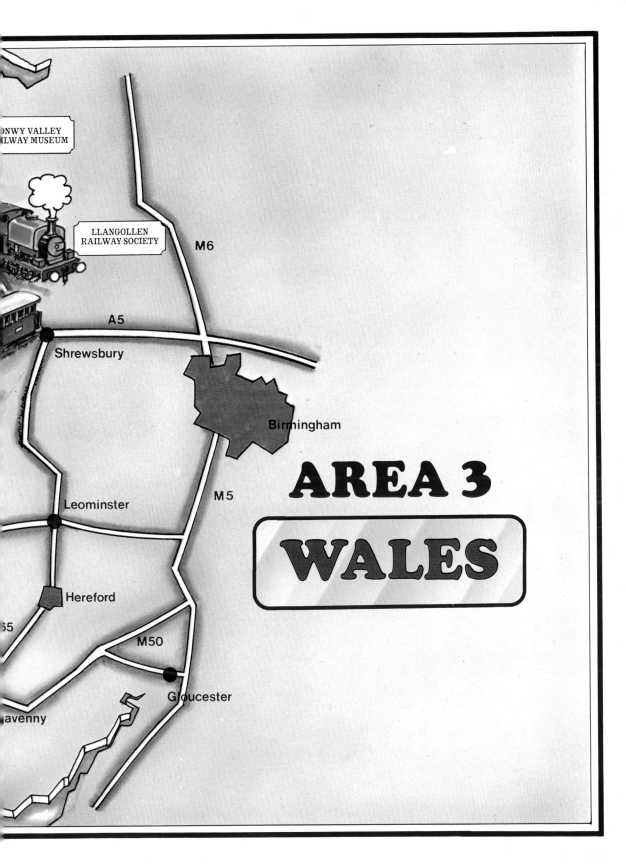

ONWY VALLEY
AILWAY MUSEUM

LLANGOLLEN
RAILWAY SOCIETY

M6

A5

Shrewsbury

Birmingham

Leominster

M5

Hereford

M50

65

Gloucester

avenny

AREA 3

WALES

Great Little Trains of Wales

Supported by the Wales Tourist Board, the narrow gauge lines of Wales have become its major tourist attraction in terms of numbers of visitors. Beginning in 1951 with the Talyllyn, the first preserved line in Britain, the railways reappeared as working systems and when there were six of them (the Snowdon always functioned and was never in danger of closure), they joined forces to market their wares. The Joint Marketing Panel was set up in 1970 and worked on the issue of a Joint Tourist Ticket allowing unlimited travel over a seven day period.

Heading for the hills. An up train leaving Tywyn on the Talyllyn Railway.

However, as more lines became members or were built new (such as the Bala Lake Railway) the 'go-as-you-please' ticket was restricted, not being accepted by the Snowdon Mountain Railway, the Great Orme Tramway, the Aberystwyth Cliff Railway and the Llechwedd Slate Caverns. The ticket is now valid for unlimited second class rides over the Talyllyn, Vale of Rheidol, Fairbourne, Festiniog, Welshpool and Llanfair, Bala Lake, and Llanberis Lake Railway. Details of train times and fares are contained in a Joint Timetable, available at the individual railways, and Tourist Information Centres. Headquarters of the Joint Marketing Panel is Wharf Station, Tywyn, Gwynedd LL36 9EY (base of the Talyllyn Railway).

Penrhyn Castle Museum

A gigantic neo-Norman castle built in 1827 by Thomas Hopper for one of the Penrhyn slate quarry owners, this structure overlooks the Menai Straits near Bangor. It is run by the National Trust, and is mainly a museum, with a huge keep modelled on that of Hedingham. Basically built of Mona marble, the castle also uses a good deal of local slate in its construction.

The museum collections include stuffed animals, butterflies and insects, plus a doll museum of national importance. For the railway enthusiast the collection of industrial locomotives will prove interesting. They all worked on Welsh slate lines, particularly the Penrhyn Railway. One or two have been restored to working order and leased to the 'Great Little Trains of Wales', while one has gone to the Lincolnshire Coast Light Railway (see page 112).

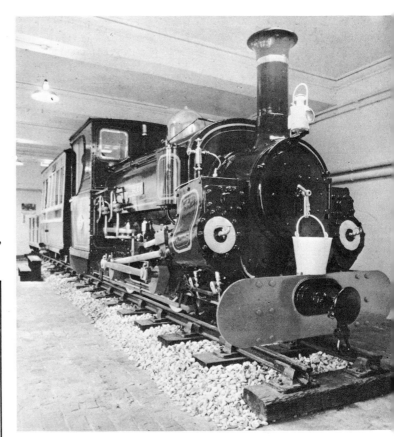

Address Penrhyn Castle Museum, Llandegai, Nr Bangor, Gwynedd, LL57 4HN. Tel. Bangor 3084

Enquiries to Above address

Opening times Daily, April to end October. 14.00 weekends, 14.00 weekdays, April, May, October. 11.00 weekdays June to September and all Bank Holidays

How to get there *By road* A5, 1 mile east of Bangor. Museum located where A5 and A55 converge. *By rail* to Bangor BR

Facilities Car park, refreshments

Discounts Children half-price

ABOVE Hunslet 0–4–0 saddle tank *Charles*, built in 1882.

FAR LEFT Hudswell Clarke 0–4–0 saddle tank *Vesta*, built in 1916.

LEFT De Winton vertical boiler *Watkin*, built in 1893.

Vale of Rheidol Railway

The Rheidol is one of seven streams rising on that great bleak mass of mountain soaked in rain and legend which the Welsh call Plynlimmon. It shares its birthplace with the Severn, but soon turns in the opposite direction and flows westwards into Cardigan Bay at Aberystwyth, having created a famed beauty spot on the way at Devil's Bridge (Pontarfynach in Welsh).

To bring sightseers and holidaymakers to Devil's Bridge, some 12 miles inland from Aberystwyth, and also to carry goods and mineral traffic, a narrow gauge railway was built in 1902 by a private company. The gauge of 1ft 11½in was identical to that of the Festiniog further north. There have been changes of ownership, from the Vale of Rheidol Company to the Cambrian in 1913, to the Great Western Railway in 1923, and to British Railways in 1948.

Today the Vale of Rheidol line is the last section of British Railways to be worked entirely by steam, and is the only narrow gauge in possession of the State organisation. British Rail has, in fact, improved facilities on this outpost of theirs, bringing the little trains into the main station of Aberystwyth back in 1966, while a new blue colour scheme for engines and coaches appeared in 1967.

From the seaside terminal the trains must climb for just over 11¾ miles up the valley to reach a height of 680ft at Devil's Bridge. A six-coach train, fully loaded as most of the Vale of Rheidol summer departures are, takes just over an hour to climb inland and just under an hour to return to the coast. For most travellers who enjoy steam train rides, the journey up is the essential trip, with all the strenuous puffing of a climb; coming downhill the engine can hardly be heard at all and it is the brakes which do all the work.

There are stations at Llanbadarn, Capel Bangor, and Abertffrwd before reaching Devil's Bridge, and a more recent halt can prove useful at Rheidol Falls. Some passengers choose to alight here, take a picnic, and walk onwards to Devil's Bridge to catch a return train. There is no fare reduction for this, but it does offer a chance to hike around some remote and splendid scenery, and gives the opportunity to photograph labouring trains from the lineside. The line is on a rocky ledge for the last 4½ miles, and another waterfall, where the River Mynach plunges 400ft near Devil's Bridge, is a highlight.

There are three engines working on the Vale of Rheidol, the only ones which

No. 7, 2–6–2 tank Owain Glyndwr on the fast stretch known as Cwmseiri between Capel Bangor and Nantyrowen.

No. 9, 2–6–2 tank *Prince of Wales* stops for water on the Vale of Rheidol Railway.

remained on the stock list of British Railways when standard gauge steam ended officially on that system in August 1968. They are all 2–6–2 tank engines, the oldest, *Prince of Wales,* dating from the opening of the line in 1902 (it was built by Davies & Metcalfe near Manchester). The other two, *Owain Glyndwr* and *Llywelyn,* are Great Western products from Swindon Works in 1923. Welsh spellings were decided on a few years ago, which meant recasting the name plates.

Since 1931 the line has been entirely dependent upon tourism; mineral workings having ceased. It continues to be prosperous, hauling about 200,000 passengers in a good summer, with services working from Easter to the end of September, ranging from one to four trains a day. Excellent facilities are maintained at Devil's Bridge. Aberystwyth has same station linkage with standard gauge Cambrian Coast and Shrewsbury trains.

There are sixteen bogie coaches to make up trains, seven of them closed, seven of them open observation vehicles, and two of them brake-composites. The dozen wagons no longer haul minerals but are used for maintenance purposes. All the equipment belongs to British Railways but the Vale of Rheidol Supporters' Association owns a camping coach once belonging to the London and North Western Railway which is positioned at Aberystwyth.

Ranking with the Festiniog and the Talyllyn as the most important of the

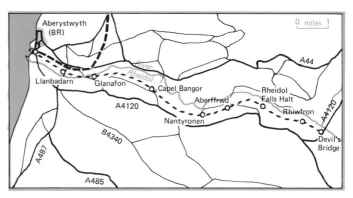

'Great Little Trains of Wales' and marketed through that organisation, the Vale of Rheidol appears to have a secure future and is a major contributor to the tourist attractions of Wales.

Address Vale of Rheidol Railway, Aberystwyth Station, Aberystwyth, Dyfed. Tel. Aberystwyth 612377

Enquiries to Above address. Timetable available

Opening times Daily, Easter to October, 10.00–17.35

How to get there *By road* A487 coast road to Aberystwyth. *By rail* to Aberystwyth BR

Facilities Car parks and refreshments at Aberystwyth and Devil's Bridge. Souvenir shop and railway letter service at Devil's Bridge

Discounts On application

Welshpool and Llanfair Railway

Welshpool and Llanfair
Railway Letter Stamp.

Famed as one of the 'Great Little Trains of Wales', the Welshpool and Llanfair is 'odd man out' as a non-coastal, non-mountain line in rather remote, pastoral, upland country. Its business has not been greatly helped by the fact that until this year it did not run between the places in its title, but from Llanfair Caereinion to Sylfaen, 5.3 miles.

Its 2ft 6in gauge tracks are now being extended into Welshpool proper, where a new station is almost complete in Raven Square, about ¾ mile from the British Rail station (trains serving this point are on the Shrewsbury to the Cambrian coast line). The full length run will be 8¾ miles, and will take about 45 minutes allowing for stops at Castle Caerinion and Sylfaen.

This sturdy little narrow gauge railway opened in 1903 to allow the inhabitants of the small country town of Llanfair Caereinion to visit Welshpool. It was built by the financially unhappy Cambrian Railway in 1903. In 1923, the Great

Western Railway, that public-spirited line which made its profits by providing genuine service to people, took over the Welshpool and Llanfair and kept it for freight from 1931 to Nationalisation. British Railways closed it in 1956, but it is to their credit that they allowed it to operate for eight years. They did not foresee the obvious attraction of such a fascinating line, restored for passenger work. A preservation society did, though, and trains began running again on the western section of the line in 1963. The Welshpool and Llanfair Light Railway Preservation Co Ltd managed to purchase the freehold of the line from BR in 1974.

The gradients are fierce, expecially the one on the newly restored sector out from Raven Square up to a summit near Sylfaen. As the Preservation Company points out, this means powerful little engines, acquired from some of the most unlikely places – but then, 2ft 6in gauge is not found universally. The Austrian Ziller-

No. 12 Kerr Stuart 0–6–2
tank *Joan* at Llanfair with
Sierre Leone Railway
coaches.

talbahn (Jenbach to Mayrhofen in the Tyrol) has been linked by loans of coaches and the supply of a powerful steam locomotive. One engine, called *Joan,* was bought from the West Indies (a sugar line). A whole train came from West Africa, from the Sierra Leone Railway running from Freetown to Waterloo.

As with most preserved railways, much of the work and operation is done by volunteers under a professional General Manager. This line was lucky to have had the help of the Royal Engineers on an exercise to replace a girder viaduct in 1965.

The two original engines are still with the railway, handsome 0–6–0 tanks built by Beyer Peacock in 1903 and named *The Earl* and *The Countess.* The Great Western gave them a major overhaul at Swindon Works in 1929, changing their appearance and adding brass embellishments. Traffic has increased greatly in recent years and at least half a dozen more engines are at work, including a large articulated locomotive called *Monarch,* built in Stafford in 1953. There are one or two diesels for track maintenance and general duties.

The Welshpool and Llanfair ride is a very pretty one, extremely rural, rising to a height of 600ft above sea level. There are good views of the River Banwy, and perhaps too many views of the A458 road which more or less follows the course of the line and is busy with traffic.

It takes a certain effort to reach this splendid little railway, unless one is driving to the Welsh coast, but it is well worth it.

At present, trains are joined at the railway headquarters, Llanfair Caereinion station, and a round trip is sold. But with the late summer opening of Welshpool Raven Square, it is expected the railway will transfer a good deal of its business to the bigger town, and will certainly sell one way and return tickets. There will be linking buses from BR trains for the short ride through the streets of Welshpool to the new W & L station.

The line will never return to its original terminus, a small yard close to the Great Western station in Welshpool. Trains used to have to negotiate narrow streets to reach Raven Square and comparatively open ground. The story is told of an unscheduled Saturday working for enthusiasts in 1956 just before closure, when the train was held up on its passage through Welshpool by many lines of washing hung across the tracks!

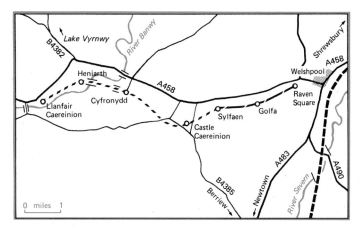

No. 1 Beyer Peacock 0–6–0 tank *The Earl,* one of the Welshpool and Llanfair's original engines.

Address The Welshpool and Llanfair Light Railway Preservation Co Ltd, The Station, Llanfair Caereinion, Powys SY21 0SF. Tel. Llanfair Caereinion 441

Enquiries to Above address. Timetable available

Opening times Daily, Easter to October (train operation), weekends open for inspection at any time

How to get there *By road* 4 miles west of Welshpool on A458. Crosville bus from Welshpool. *By rail* to Welshpool BR. Connecting bus (infrequent)

Discounts Family tickets and party rates. Children half-price

Facilities Car park, refreshments and souvenir shop at Llanfair Caereinion. Car park opposite Castle Caereinion Station, off B4385

Festiniog Railway

ABOVE Festiniog Railway Letter Stamps.

RIGHT Hunslet 2–4–0 saddle tank *Blanche* arriving at Tan-y-Bwlch.

BELOW Alco 2–6–2 tank *Mountaineer* by Porthmadog Harbour.

If railways are your pleasure, and narrow gauge ones a special delight, then there is a particular line that must not be missed on any visit to North Wales. The world-famous Festiniog, a unique line, is probably the oldest narrow gauge railway in the world, and now one that has captured the public imagination in its fight against financial, topographical and bureaucratic odds, to succeed beyond the wildest dreams of its creator.

The Festiniog Railway was constructed in 1836 by a Mr James Spooner. The gauge was only 60cm or 1ft 11½in, the narrowest ever laid in the first 50 years of world railway construction. The objective was to bring slate down from the great quarries around Blaenau Festiniog to the sea at what was then called (and spelt) Portmadoc, and it was an instant success. Gravity brought the loaded waggons down and horses hauled the empty ones uphill. The horses returned to the seaport as passengers in a special waggon attached to the back of the train.

Charles Easton Spooner took over as engineer of the line after the death of his father in 1856, and soon saw that traffic

was growing too heavy for horses to continue handling. By 1863, steam engines had been delivered, and by 1865, the Board of Trade gave permission for human passengers to be carried – the first time this had been granted to a line in Britain narrower than 4ft 8½in. A designer named Fairlie became world-famous for creating double-ended articulated locomotives, and the first one, called *Little Wonder,* was tremendously successful. In 1879 the Festiniog managed to build, in its shops at Boston Lodge, a Fairlie double-ender of its own, named *Merddin Emrys.* Last year this superb veteran celebrated its centenary and is still strong enough to haul passenger trains up the line today. By 1981 it will probably head the first train right into the new Blaenau Festiniog station.

Despite its fame, *Merddin Emrys* is not

the oldest engine on the line. *Prince* and *Princess,* both single-enders, actually 0–4–0 saddle tanks with tenders, date from the very beginning of steam on the Festiniog and are thus each 117 years old. There are plenty of other steam locomotives in use today, acquired from various sources or retained from the Festiniog's early period. Fairly recent is a 0–6–0 saddle tank built by Pecketts in 1944, while there are several diesels. One of these handles the winter weekend trains.

Probably the most modern steam locomotive in the world built for passenger traffic was put into service by the Festiniog in 1979. It is the 'double-ender', *Earl of Merioneth,* built in the Boston Lodge works of the railway, with the latest equipment yet to a design more than a hundred years old. This should ensure safe steaming well into the 21st century.

CENTRE LEFT Hunslet 2–4–0 saddle tank *Linda.*

RIGHT Her 'sister' *Blanche.* The famous double-ender, *Merddin Emrys.*

In all the railway has 11 steam and 7 diesel engines, and 27 passenger vehicles. The rolling stock ranges between such extremes as knife-board box-like carriages from 1864 and a saloon buffet coach built in 1897, while there are a fair number of quite modern coaches, including smooth riding bogies, from the 1964–72 period.

The fight to restore the Festiniog Railway, on which desultory passenger services ended with the outbreak of the Second World War in 1939, has been a long and hard one. Inspired by the success of preservationists on the Talyllyn Railway only 30 miles away, a Festiniog Railway Society was formed in June 1954. Gradually, with a tremendous amount of enthusiastic voluntary labour, services were resumed, and Tan-y-Bwlch was reached by 1958. This gave thousands of holidaymakers a pleasant and scenic journey, 7½ miles long.

When the Central Electricity Generating Board constructed a major power station, a considerable diversion had to be built to avoid flooding. Fortunately, after years of battling bureaucracy, compensation was obtained. By 1968, the line had got to Dduallt, and by 1977 it had rounded the works of the hydro-electric scheme, gone through a new tunnel and entered Tanygrisiau. Grants totalling £177,000 have come from the Manpower Services Commission, the Wales Tourist Board and the National Westminster Bank.

Now 12 miles long, the railway has 1½ miles to go to enter Blaenau Ffestiniog (the correct Welsh spelling), where a new joint station is being built. This will allow connection with the British Rail branch to Llandudno. At present a bus connection is provided, offering an excursion mostly by train from Cardigan Bay to the Liverpool Bay.

The uphill ride is magnificent, starting from Porthmadog, then crossing a causeway to Boston Lodge works, where the climbing begins in earnest. The narrow gauge rails cling to mountainsides as the train heads up into the heart of Snowdonia. The ride to Tanygrisiau takes about 70 minutes.

Address Festiniog Railway Company, Porthmadog, Gwynedd. Tel. Porthmadog 2384

Enquiries to Above address. Timetable available

Opening times All year, weekends November to end March, daily end March to beginning November, 09.15 to close of operations

How to get there *By road* A487 coast road. Crosville bus to Porthmadog, Tan-y-Bwlch and Minfford. *By rail* to BR Porthmadog, Minfford, or Blaenau Ffestiniog

Facilities Car park, refreshments at Porthmadog, Tan-y-Bwlch and Tanygrisiau and souvenir shop

Special attractions Model Railway Centre and Museum at Porthmadog. Picnic site and Nature Trail at Tan-y-Bwlch

Discounts For groups of 25 or more. Children half-price

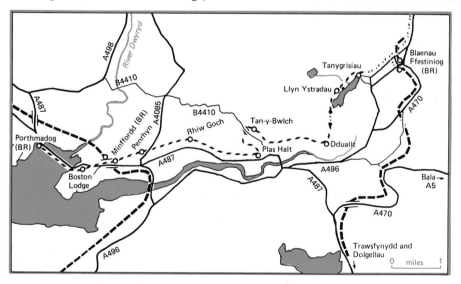

Great Orme Tramway

Llandudno in North Wales and East-bourne in East Sussex were built as sister resorts in late Victorian times, similarly architectured and with parallel holiday facilities. Few alterations have marred their elegance to this day, and both enjoy long seaside promenades with well maintained piers. At one time, each resort had a pleasure tramway, the one at Eastbourne running eastwards over the Crumbles towards St Leonards (it is now moved in its entirety to South Devon) rather than up the steep incline to Beachy Head, while Llandudno's was built up the grade to that resort's 'home cliff', Great Orme Head.

The Great Orme Tramway survives in virtually the same condition that it was in at the opening in 1903. Built to a gauge of 3 ft 6 in, it climbs in two sections from Victoria Station in the centre of Llandudno, using electrically driven cable traction (steam powered in its early years). It was owned by the Great Orme Railway Company until 1949 when it passed into the control of the Urban District Council.

The lower section is $\frac{1}{2}$ mile long up a maximum gradient of 1 in 4.4, a ride which takes about 8 minutes. Passengers must change cars at the half-way point.

The upper section is also $\frac{1}{2}$ mile long with a maximum gradient of 1 in 10.3, and like the lower section is single track with a passing loop. The total journey takes just under 20 minutes, with a service of cars operating every 20 minutes throughout the summer season.

There are four tramcars, each seating forty-eight passengers. The tramway is marketed with the 'Great Little Trains of Wales'. The terminal station is fractionally below the 649 ft summit of Great Orme Head, where a restaurant and shop are located. Down in the resort, ample parking is available close to Church Walks adjacent to Victoria Station.

Address Great Orme Tramway, Llandudno Urban District Council, Transport Dept, Builder St West, Llandudno. Tel. 76749

Enquiries to Above address

Opening times 1st May to 4th October, peak season services between 1st July and 31st August, 10.00–18.00 (21.00 peak season)

How to get there *By road* to centre of Llandudno, A546. *By rail* to BR Llandudno Junction, then by various Crosville buses

Facilities Parking available close Victoria Station, restaurant and shop on Great Orme Head

Discounts Reduced rate for children

The Great Orme Tramway in Llandudno.

Snowdon Mountain Railway

One of the Snowdon
Mountain Railway's seven
0–4–2 tank engines.

Built in 1896 as Britain's only rack railway, the $4\frac{3}{4}$-mile long Snowdon Summit line is exactly as it was at the turn of the century. Then, as now, it owned seven specially built rack and pinion steam tank engines from Switzerland and nine passenger carriages. But three of the engines date from the 1920s.

Based on the ABT system (there are two other rack methods for hauling up steep climbs), the Winterthur-built engines engage two jaggedly-toothed tracks laid in the centre of the permanent way. Speed on the Snowdon is necessarily slow (around 5 miles per hour): about the same as the Mount Washington Cogwheel Railway in New Hampshire (the world's first) and the Vitznau-Rigi in Switzerland (the

world's second). The stiffest gradient is 1 in $5\frac{1}{2}$, after Clogwyn passing place.

This British 2ft $7\frac{1}{2}$in line climbs from Llanberis station to the Snowdon Summit, the top station being at 3,500ft, just 60ft below the actual summit marker. Llanberis station is 353ft above sea level so the railway climbs 3,207ft in the course of its run. Journey time is one hour, and trains consist of one engine pushing up one carriage with a maximum capacity of sixty persons per departure. This leads to long queues on fine days.

The only accident was on opening day, Easter Monday, 1896, when engine No. 1, *Ladas*, derailed and plunged from a precipice. The carriage was not affected, however. No other mishap has occurred in its 84 years of operation.

Although considered one of the most important of the 'Great Little Trains of Wales' and marketed through that organisation, the Snowdon Mountain Railway is not worked or helped by enthusiasts or preservationists. It is a limited company with an entirely professional staff. As with all difficult mountain lines anywhere the price of the ride tends to be high, the fare having to take into account that in bad weather no trains run. This can include days of good visibility but severe winds, while on fine days demand is so great that extra trains must be put on and a good deal of overtime worked.

The seven 0–4–2 tank engines all have Welsh names. There is no No. 1, since that was *Ladas*, lost so long ago, but Nos. 2 to 8 are named: *Enid, Wyddfa, Snowdon, Moel Siabond, Padarn, Aylwin* and *Eryri*. No diesels are operated by the railway.

Obviously, the rail trip up Snowdon is a highly desirable outing for anyone visiting this part of North Wales, but due to the high cost it is essential to choose a fine day. For those keen on walking and reasonably experienced on mountain hikes, some money can be saved by riding up and walking down. The track, close to the line, is safe enough and easy going on a fine clear day. But weather conditions change abruptly on the Snowdon ridges.

Once the train has puffed exhausted into the Summit station it is worth reflecting that it is *exactly one-quarter as high* as a similar rack railway built around the same time with Swiss influence in America. This is the Pike's Peak Railway into the high Rockies from Colorado Springs, which was steam operated for its first 60 years, although Swiss-built diesel railcars now handle the climb to 14,000 ft.

Address Snowdon Mountain Railway Ltd, Llanberis, Gywnedd, LL55 47Y. Tel. Llanberis 223

Enquiries to General Manager, at above address. Timetable available

Opening times Daily, May to October, 09.00–17.00

How to get there *By road* A4086 Caernarvon to Betws-y-Coed. *By rail* to Bangor BR, then bus from station

Facilities Car park, restaurant, snack bar and shop at Llanberis. Restaurant, bar and shop at the Summit station

Discounts For groups of 25 or more. Children half-price

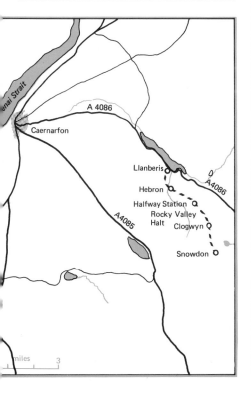

TOP Clogwyn passing place.

CENTRE No. 4 *Snowdon,* built in 1896, at Llanberis.

LEFT Spectacular views from Summit Station, at 3,500 ft.

Welsh Highland Light Railway

The once-bustling slate port of Porthmadog at the northern end of Cardigan Bay had two narrow gauge railways in the 1920s and 1930s. One of them, the Festiniog, is virtually fully restored and functioning. The other, the Welsh Highland Railway, failed to prosper during its short life from 1923 to 1936, and was dismantled before the War.

However, strenuous and long drawn-out efforts by members of the Welsh Highland Light Railway Ltd have resulted in a start being made to put some of this superbly scenic 1 ft 11½ in line back in working order. It will be a most welcome addition to the growing list of 'Great Little Trains of Wales'.

In 1978, the Gwynedd County Council finally approved a scheme to reopen the Welsh Highland from Porthmadog to a point north of Beddgelert, and a job creation scheme enabled a workforce to restore Beddgelert Sidings. The objective is to reach Pont Croesor, some 3 miles from the seaport terminus. Originally the Welsh Highland climbed through some magnificent sections of Snowdonia to make contact with the former London, Midland and Scottish Railway at Caernafon.

A token service managed to function in 1979, from Porthmadog to Pen-y-Mount Halt, barely a mile. Each year should see more railway working, and on it is some historic equipment. This includes the original Welsh Highland 2–6–2 tank engine *Russell,* built in 1906 which was saved after the 1936 closure. One of the rare Orenstein & Koppel narrow gauge engines, a 0–6–0 well tank, has been brought to the line and restored. A 0–4–2 Peckett tank has been acquired from South Africa, while three other engines are being rebuilt or restored.

With public support and a good deal of voluntary labour, the Welsh Highland may yet penetrate along its old route beyond Pont Croesor in the years ahead.

Meanwhile a short ride on it at summer weekends, if visiting Porthmadog for the famous Festiniog, will be a worthy bonus. Reasonable riding conditions are assured by some fascinating rolling stock, including two former Isle of Man bogie coaches and a four-wheeled passenger brake van from the same-gauge Vale of Rheidol.

Address Welsh Highland Light Railway (1964) Ltd, Gelert's Farm Works, Madoc Street West, Porthmadog, Gwynedd, LL49 9DY. Tel. Porthmadog 3402

Enquiries to Mr C. J. Keylock, 106 Crompton Rd, Macclesfield, Cheshire. Tel. Macclesfield 26869

Opening times Every weekend

How to get there *By road* A487 coast road to Porthmadog. *By rail* to Porthmadog. Across road from BR station

Facilities Car park, refreshments and souvenir shop

RIGHT A view of the old Welsh Highland Railway, in Nantnor Cutting.

FAR RIGHT Orenstein and Koppel 0–6–0 well tank *Pedemoura,* built in 1924, on the Welsh Highland Light Railway.

Aberystwyth Cliff Railway

Conwy Valley Railway Museum

One of the longest coastal cliff lifts, this one at Aberystwyth, terminal on the Cambrian Coast for the British Rail line from Shrewsbury and of the Vale of Rheidol Railway, runs 890ft and has a vertical lift of 400ft.

The base station is Cliff Terrace and the Summit is on top of Constitution Hill. Close to the Summit Station there is a café, and various footpaths offer pleasant walks with good views over the town (which lies to the south).

Address Aberystwyth Cliff Railway Co Ltd, Cliff House, Cliff Terrace, Aberystwyth, Dyfed, SY23 2DN. Tel. Aberystwyth 61742

Enquiries to Traffic manager, at above address

Opening times Easter, and May to September inclusive, 10.00–18.00, 10.00–21.00 high season. Departures every 5 to 7 minutes

How to get there *By road* to Lower Station, Aberystwyth. *By rail* to Aberystwyth BR, ½ mile away

Facilities Car park, refreshments and souvenir shop

Discounts For groups of 20 or more. Reduced rate for children

In the shadow of Snowdonia lies the attractive little town of Betws-y-coed, an intermediate station on the diesel unit pay-train route between Llandudno and Blaenau Ffestiniog. No freight trains operate on this line any more, so the goods yard at Betws-y-coed became redundant. The site was cleared by British Railways who allowed the Conwy Valley Railway Museum to acquire it.

Some static standard gauge exhibits stand in the open but inside a new museum building are numerous models covering a wide period. There is a good deal of emphasis on the 'Great Little Trains of Wales' but at the same time, the former importance of standard gauge branch lines in Wales is not overlooked. Various items of signalling equipment are displayed, as well as small items such as buttons and cutlery from 120 different railway companies. Large scale locomotive models are contrasted with some 'toys' from the 1920s.

On the track outside stands a fairly modern buffet car, which dispenses refreshments to visitors. There are two small steam locomotives to be seen, but steamings are not held.

Best access is by train to adjacent Betws-y-coed station after an extremely scenic ride up the Conwy Valley.

Address Conwy Valley Railway Museum, Old Goods Yard, Betws-y-coed, Gwynedd, LL24 0AL. Tel. Betws-y-coed 568

Enquiries to Above address

Opening times Daily mid-April to end September, weekends in October

How to get there *By road* A5, Llangollen to Bangor. *By rail* to Betws-y-Coed BR, museum adjacent to station

Facilities Car park, buffet car and souvenir shop

Special attractions Steam Miniature Railway

Talyllyn Railway

RIGHT No. 2 Fletcher Jennings 0–4–0 well tank *Dolgoch* at Rhydyronen, oldest intermediate station on the line.

BELOW No. 4 Kerr Stuart 0–4–2 saddle tank *Edward Thomas* on an up train.

To this 2ft 3in gauge slate quarry railway, owned and operated by Sir Henry Haydn Jones, Liberal M.P. for so many years, goes the honour of being the first in the world to be preserved and restored by railway enthusiasts. If the project, started a year after Sir Henry's death in 1950, had not succeeded, it is highly improbable that any of the great number of railways for pleasure would be running today.

But succeed it did and the Talyllyn can claim happily that its services have been operating continuously since 1866. There was never a break, although in 1951 only one locomotive was operational, the rolling stock was in a badly decayed condition and the track was rotten. The Talyllyn Railway Preservation Society, formed with the help of the executors of Sir Henry Haydn Jones, quickly got to work

with large numbers of volunteers. By 1957 there were four engines functioning, two Talyllyn originals *(Talyllyn* and *Dolgoch)* plus two 0–4–2 saddle tanks acquired from the former Corris Railway, one of which was named *Sir Haydn* to revere the name of the man who, out of his own pocket, had kept the railway running so long.

Today the railway has actually been extended beyond its latter day limits, from 6½ miles to 7¼ miles. It owns six steam engines and three small diesels, although only five of the former are rostered for traffic. There are 20 well maintained coaches for passenger traffic, some of them built quite recently. In addition, there are a considerable number of goods wagons.

The starting point is Tywyn (pronounced and previously spelt 'Towyn') on Cardigan Bay, at the modernized Wharf Station, a comparatively short walk from the British Rail station on the Shrewsbury-Pwllheli Cambrian Coast line. There is the fine Narrow Gauge Railway Museum adjoining the Wharf with exhibits drawn from all over Britain, including seven steam locomotives but also displaying smaller items down to uniform buttons. It is run by a charitable trust and staffed by volunteers.

Address Talyllyn Railway, Wharf Station, Tywyn, Gwynedd LL36 9EY. Tel. Tywyn 710472

Enquiries to Traffic Department, at above address. Timetable available

Opening times March to October, limited service at Christmas. Frequent daily service between 7th April and 4th November. See timetable for details.

How to get there *By road* A493 Aberdovey to Dolgellau. Line runs beside B4405, Tywyn to Talyllyn Lake. Crosville bus. *By rail* to Tywyn BR

Facilities Large car park near Wharf Station, car parks at Dolgoch Falls and Abergynolwyn, refreshments, souvenir shop. Booking office for passengers not riding whole length of line at Abergynolwyn

Special attractions Narrow Gauge Railway Museum at Wharf Station

Discounts For groups of 25 or more. Children half-price

TOP A down train hauled by No. 3, Hughes 0–4–2 saddle tank *Sir Haydn.*

CENTRE Double-header: No. 1 Fletcher Jennings 0–4–2 saddle tank *Talyllyn* leads *Edward Thomas* on a busy up train.

LEFT *Dolgoch* with an up train in Rhydyronen.

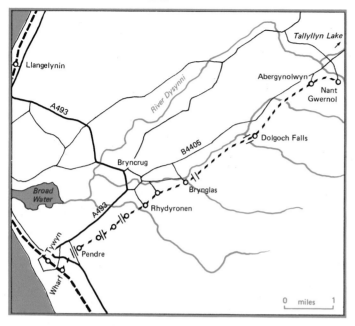

That American railroad folk hero Casey Jones, about whom so many songs and ballads (all inaccurate) have been written, has his counterpart on this famous Welsh narrow gauge. The Talyllyn driver's name was Hyw ap Sion (which is approximate Welsh for Casey Jones). The stanzas of the ballad have built up over the years, but a keen Talyllyn volunteer named Desmond Martin gives the following extract:

'Hyw ap Sion steaming down the valley,
Hyw ap Sion going by Fach Goch,
Hyw ap Sion whistling for the crossing,
Coupling at Pendre onto empty stock.

He ran around at Wharf upon that fateful day,
Collected the staff and got the rightaway,
then roared up through the cutting past Pendre
    and by Ty-Mawr
Set on Nant Gwernol in half an hour' . . .

Needless to say, Hyw's train met another
    face to face:

'Hyw said just before he died,
There's two more roads I would like to ride.
The fireman said they can only be
The old Gorsedda and Hendre-Ddu.

Hyw ap Sion driving through the cloud wrack,
Hyw ap Sion with an angel band,
Hyw ap Sion standing on the footplate
of a narrow gauge engine in the Promised Land'.

ABOVE Talyllyn Railway Letter Stamp.

RIGHT Barclay 0–4–0 well tank *Douglas* with an up train at Dolgoch Falls.

The route through the Fathew Valley is spectacular, passing ledges, ravines and forests. Cader Idris is in view to the left of an ascending train, while Taren Hendre can be seen to the right and dead ahead lies Tarenygesall, all mountains well above 2,000ft. Just before Dolgoch station the line passes close to the Dolgoch Falls, a noted beauty spot. The last 2 miles are through very wild country, along a narrowing valley to Abergynolwyn, former terminus of the railway, then steeply uphill to Nant Gwernol, opened in May 1976. This can only be reached by train or on foot.

Trains take about 55 minutes to make the $7\frac{1}{4}$ uphill miles, and the round trip including switching arrangements at Nant Gwernol takes about $2\frac{1}{4}$ hours. Lucky travellers will ride behind either *Talyllyn* or *Dolgoch*, built in 1865 and 1866 respectively, thoroughly rebuilt but retaining their original appearance. Engine No. 4, *Edward Thomas,* an 0–4–2 saddle tank of 1879 from the Corris Railway, was fitted with an oblong Giesel Ejector by the famous Dr Giesl-Gieslingen of Vienna in 1958, improving the engine's performance by over a third.

The Talyllyn Railway, one of the top tourist attractions of Wales and a member of the 'Great Little Trains', carries over 100,000 passengers a year.

Gwili Railway

This is a standard gauge short line designed to appeal to railway enthusiasts in West Wales and holidaymakers spending their time at resorts around the coast of what used to be Pembrokeshire and in the southern parts of Cardigan Bay.

Called in Welsh, Cymni Rheilffordd Gwili Cwf, the line is heavily supported by the Wales Tourist Board which is delighted to have the real 'big' thing in a country with so many narrow gauge lines. But it is a Railway Company, having been formed in 1975 with a share capital of £100,000. It preserves a short section of the former Carmarthen to Aberystwyth line and starts from Bronwydd Arms station, about 2 miles north of Carmarthen on the A484 road.

The present run is only about 1½ miles to Cwmdwyfran, but negotiations are still proceeding to get rights over about 8 miles of track, largely beside the Gwili River as far as Llanpumpsaint, starting from Abergwili Junction, south from Bronwydd Arms. Within two years there may be a considerable advance along the restored track which will make the Gwili one of the very worthwhile steam trips in Britain. Meanwhile the run lasts only 8 minutes each way.

The project is supported locally by the Gwili Railway Preservation Society, which does not possess any locomotives or rolling stock although it has organized several rail tours over the line and elsewhere.

Three steam engines belong to the Gwili Company, a former Great Western Prairie tank, and two saddle tanks from industrial lines, one a 0–4–0 and the other a 0–6–0. There is a Wickham diesel car for line workings, and three typical GWR branch line carriages. All stock is at Bronwydd Arms station.

0–4–0 Peckett saddle tank Merlin/Myrddin out in the country approaching Cwmwyfran with a train from Bronwydd Arms.

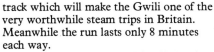

Address Gwili Railway Co Ltd, Bronwydd Arms, Nr Carmarthen, Dyfed

Enquiries to Great Western Chambers, Angel St, Neath, SA11 1RS. Tel. Neath 2191. Timetable available

Opening times Bank Holidays, weekends July–September, weekdays (vary) end July to end August, Saturdays 13.00–17.00, Sundays 12.00–17.30, Bank Holidays 11.00–17.30

How to get there *By road* A484, right at Bronwydd sign. *By rail* to Carmarthen BR (2½ miles) then Crosville bus

Facilities Car park, refreshments and souvenir shop at 'Bronwydd Arms'

Discounts For groups. Reduced rate for children

Fairbourne Railway

One of the original six 'Great Little Trains of Wales', the Fairbourne is only 15 in gauge, one of three active steam operated passenger-carrying railways using that gauge in the British Isles. It dates from 1916 when a subsidiary of the famous model-makers Bassett-Lowke Ltd converted a former horse-drawn tramway working a ferry link at Barmouth.

The present company running the Fairbourne started in 1947 and operate it seriously and professionally over $2\frac{1}{4}$ miles of track between Fairbourne Station on the vital Cambrian Coast Line of British Railways and a halt at Penrhyn Point where the ferry to Barmouth starts.

BELOW Guest 2–4–2 *Sian* on the Fairbourne Railway.

The ride takes about twenty minutes, with calls at two halts (Bathing Beach and Golf House), and is more or less level, with superb views to Snowdonia and across the wide Mawddach Estuary (which is not crossed by a road bridge, only the Cambrian rail viaduct). Little steam engines and comfortable carriages (open or closed according to weather and as presentable as those on the much longer Romney, Hythe and Dymchurch – see page 30) make this a fascinating trip for everyone, young and old, and useful, too, for those taking the ferry.

Pride of the line is the Bassett-Lowke Atlantic (4–4–2) built in 1924 and named

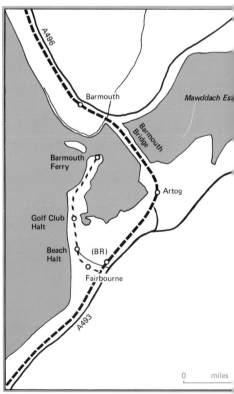

LEFT Bassett-Lowke Atlantic 4–4–2 *Count Louis*.

BELOW Fairbourne's 4–6–2 *Ernest W. Twining* heads a well-loaded train.

Count Louis after Count Louis Zborowski, an Edwardian racing motorist and railway enthusiast. The biggest engine is *Ernest W. Twining*, a 4–6–2, dating from 1949 but rebuilt in the 1966–67 off-season. Two other smaller steam engines and some miniature diesels (mainly for track work) complete the roster.

Address Fairbourne Railway Ltd, Beach Rd, Fairbourne, Gwynedd, LL38 2EX. Tel. Fairbourne 250362

Enquiries to Above address. Timetable available

Opening times Easter week; Sundays, April to end May; daily end May to mid-October. Usually 10.30 first train, 17.00 last train. High season 10.00 first, 17.30–18.00 last

How to get there *By road* A493 between Dolgellau and Tywyn. Crossville bus No. S28. *By rail* to Fairbourne BR, adjacent to the Railway

Facilities Car park, refreshments and souvenir shop

Special attractions Ferry link to Barmouth

Discounts Weekly party season available on request. Out of season, special party, etc., rates. Children half-price

Caerphilly Railway Society

Brecon Mountain Railway

Once the locomotive works of the former Rhymney Railway, a coal hauling constituent of the Great Western, the Caerphilly Society's headquarters are now part of the Harold Wilson Industrial Estate. There is access for the public only on steaming days, which take place about six times between April and September and are locally advertised.

The Society has about half a dozen steam locomotives, five of which are being fully restored to working order on behalf of the National Museum of Wales. The important one, which brings the majority of visitors (and it is stressed that small groups can come by prior arrangement outside the steaming days) is a fomer Taff Vale Railway 0–6–2 tank, built in 1897. Numbered 28, the engine passed to the National Coal Board from the GWR, and was presented to the National Museum in 1962, believed to be the only surviving standard gauge Welsh-built locomotive in preservation.

The Brecon Mountain Railway does not yet exist as a functioning railway, although it is considerably aided by the Wales Tourist Board as part of its industrial archaeology visitor programme for South Wales and its hinterland. An entirely new 2ft gauge line is to be built from Pontsticill Junction on the former Brecon and Merthyr railway, running for no less than 8 miles through the grandeur of the Brecon Beacons.

Engines and rolling stock are being assembled at Pontsticill, including imports from abroad, especially South Africa (where 2ft gauge tracks exist in profusion in Natal and Eastern Cape Province). These may be seen, stored.

It is intended that a section of the old Brecon and Merthyr Canal should be restored as part of the visitor attraction.

Address Caerphilly Railway Society Ltd, Harold Wilson Industrial Estate, Van Road, Caerphilly, Mid Glamorgan
Enquiries to Publicity Officer, at above address
Opening times Open days in steam as advertised in local press
How to get there *By road* A468 from Newport. *By rail* to Caerphilly BR
Facilities Refreshments
Discounts Children half-price

Address Brecon Mountain Railway Co Ltd, Pontsticill Station, Merthyr Tydfil, Mid Glamorgan, CF48 2UP. Tel. Merthyr Tydfil 4854
Enquiries to Above address
How to get there *By road* Off A465 Abergavenny to Neath. *By rail* to Merthyr Tydfil BR
Facilities Car park, refreshments and souvenir shop

Llechwedd Slate Caverns

Not a railway in the strict sense of the term, this is an important tourist attraction in North Wales, close to the Festiniog Railway's route, and has been a recipient of a major British Tourist Authority award.

A battery-powered electric train-tram takes visitors from the surface on the outskirts of Blaenau Ffestiniog down into a restored slate quarry. The scene shows how slate workers quarried the product during the heyday of Welsh slate at the turn of the century, with working examples in various sections. A new Incline Railway, designed to take passengers to deeper levels, opened in 1979.

Address Llechwedd Slate Caverns, Blaenau Ffestiniog, Gwynedd, LL41 3NB. Tel. Blaenau Ffestiniog 306

Enquiries to Above address. Timetable available

Opening times Daily, March 1st to end October. Train-trams run 10.00–17.15 – a tour lasting just under an hour

How to get there *By road* A470 1 mile north of Blaenau Ffestiniog. *By rail* to Blaenau Ffestiniog BR, then bus

Facilities Free parking for cars and coaches, café and slate souvenir shop (also selling Welsh craft gifts)

Discounts For groups of 20 or more. Reduced rate for OAPs and children

ABOVE Llechwedd Railway Letter Stamps: note the unique postmark.

LEFT The new Incline Railway. Britain's steepest underground passenger incline.

FAR LEFT The Miners' Tramway takes visitors down into Llechwedd Slate Caverns. On the left is a tableau recreating Victorian working conditions there.

81

Llanberis Lake Railway

Strictly speaking, the Llanberis Lake Railway (or Rheilffordd Llyn Llanberis as it is in Welsh) is a railway built for pleasure, and built fairly recently as a new addition to the veteran 'Great Little Trains of Wales'.

It is a company formed with the help of a local railway society and financial assistance from the Wales Tourist Board which laid tracks along the bed of the old Padarn Railway. Building began in 1971, just two years after the liquidation of Dinorwic slate quarries, the largest of their kind in the world. The first section of line was constructed with track from the Dinorwic works, and it then follows the route of the Padarn, but only for 2 miles, the limit of the new railway.

The gauge decided upon is 1 ft 11½ in, the same as that of the Festiniog, although the original Padarn gauge was much wider. However, some small engines from the quarries were 1 ft 11½ in and a few industrial diesels of that gauge were available. Carriages were built specially for the railway, some enclosed and some partially open.

The route is almost at right angles to that of the Snowdon, which leaves from

Llanberis to climb the mountain. Snowdon is in full view on a fine day as the Lake Railway crosses the Afon Wen River and hugs the lake. Actual starting point in Llanberis is Gilfach Ddu station, and the terminal 2 miles away is Penllyn (head or end of the lake), but passengers must remain on board the train here although they can alight at the intermediate station of Cei Llydan, where there are fine picnic sites.

The Llanberis Lake Railway owns five steam locomotives and nine diesels, with eleven units of rolling stock, so a good service can be offered on fine summer days. It is very much more for fun-loving holidaymakers than serious railway enthusiasts, although some of the engines have excellent pedigrees especially No. 1, *Elidir*, dating from 1889. No less than 19 of the Dinorwic Quarry engines were saved in 1969 and some of them have gone to museums in Wales. The Penrhyn Castle Museum has one of them, *Fire Queen*, also an original carriage from the 1880s.

The Gilfach Ddu area is being turned into a tourist zone with a Country Park.

BELOW No. 1 Hunslet 0–4–0 saddle tank *Elidir*, built in 1889, at Gilfach Ddu.

Address Llanberis Lake Railway, Gilfach Ddu Llanberis, Gwynedd LL55 4TY. Tel. Llanberis 549

Enquiries to Commercial Manager, at above address. Timetable available

Opening times Easter to first Sunday in October, daily 10.30 to 17.30. See timetable for details

How to get there *By road* A4086 Caernarfon-Betws-y-Coed, then private approach road to station at Padarn Park. *By rail* to Bangor BR, then bus

Facilities Car parks, refreshments, souvenir shops

Special attractions Part of the Padarn Country Park complex, which combines natural, industrial and social history in one unique 'package'

Discounts For groups. Children half-price

Bala Lake Railway

There used to be a scenic main line owned by the Great Western Railway which brought holidaymakers from the north through Chester to Ruabon and then almost straight across northern Wales to Barmouth. It had served Llangollen and the Dee Valley as well as the Cambrian Coast, but was closed under the Beeching Butchery and trains ceased in 1965.

For about $4\frac{1}{2}$ miles the line skirted Bala Lake, largest body of natural fresh water in Wales. On this track bed were laid narrow gauge rails six years after main line closure, as a result of the formation of a company called Rheilffordd Llyn Tegid (Bala Lake Railway Ltd). At first only $1\frac{1}{2}$ miles were operative but by 1976 the track came close to Bala town centre, to a station on the site of the GWR's Bala Lake Halt.

This is a 'Festiniog gauge' line, 1 ft $11\frac{1}{2}$ in. It is supported by the Bala Lake Railway Society, and the Company, which decides policy and operates the trains, is financially supported by Uptonspur, a division of the Guinness Leisure empire. Built entirely for pleasure journeys and one of the newest of the 'Great Little Trains of Wales', the Bala Lake is shifting well over 50,000 holidaymakers a season.

The base of operations is Llanuwchllyn station, intact from GWR days, where the shed is located. Steam train rides are provided, and diesel as well, over the $4\frac{1}{2}$ miles travelling in a northeasterly direction to Bala, the ride taking just under half an hour if stopping at halts along the way. Apart from lovely views of the Bala Lake, there are mountains all around, with peaks in the 2,800 to 2,925 ft range. Cader Idris, a famous mountain, is visible shortly before the train enters Bala station.

Three steam engines work on the line, including the diminutive *Maid Marian* formerly a Dinorwic Slate Quarries engine and dating from 1903. She was the only steam engine on the line up to 1976 and was supported by the 'Maid Marian Fund'. Now two other 1902 veterans built by

Hunslet have joined her, but there are ten diesels as well, one of them called *Meirionydd* shaped like a BR 'Western' class diesel hydraulic. This diesel came new to Bala in 1973. There are eight coaches, two of them open 'toast-racks'.

Address Rheilffordd Llyn Tegid (Bala Lake Railway), Yr Orsaf, Llanuwchllyn, Bala, Gwynedd. Tel. Llanuwchllyn 666, or Bala 520226

Enquiries to Above address. Timetable available

Opening times Daily, Easter to end September, weekends to mid-October. Railway staffed all year round

How to get there *By road* Off A494 Dolgellau-Bala, 5 miles south of Bala. Weekdays, Crosville bus (D94) Wrexham-Barmouth. *By rail* to Ruabon or Barmouth BR, then bus

Facilities Car park, refreshments and souvenir shop

Discounts For families or 3 adults, and OAPs. Children half-price

Lovely views of Bala Lake, with the mountains in the background.

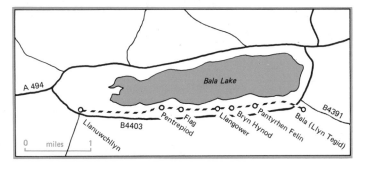

83

Llangollen Railway Society

Although it is the centre for the Welsh National Eisteddfod, Llangollen, lovely town on the banks of the Dee, has had no railway service since British Rail closed the main line of the former Great Western from Ruabon to Barmouth.

There is, however, hope for the future, for Llangollen station has been restored by a railway society and a lease obtained on the trackbed for at least 3 miles along the Dee to the border of the County of Clwyd. The Llangollen Railway Preservation Society Ltd hopes to extend its line to Corwen, some 10 miles westward. It is nearly 15 years since trains ran on this route. Tracks have been relaid in the station and it looks a picture of activity on those days when one or two engines are in steam, with rolling stock parked and people about, viewing the equipment and buying souvenirs at the station shop.

Already, the track has advanced half a mile beyond the station, and by the summer of 1980 if all goes well, a 0–6–0 saddle tank with obvious industrial origins may be hauling a coach or two on short journeys. The Shell Oil Refinery at Stanlow has been very helpful in allowing its unwanted track to be lifted and brought to Llangollen by volunteers. There is still need for more engines and rolling stock, although small industrial engines have now been made available.

Steam on the Dee will be a great tourist attraction in the years ahead, especially on a standard gauge railway in Wales where so many narrow gauge lines function. Meanwhile, anyone travelling in the area should visit Llangollen Station at a weekend in summer. There will be steam up and there may be a short scenic ride.

OPPOSITE Llangollen station, on the banks of the Dee.

BELOW Kitson 0–6–0 saddle tank *Kitson* in steam at Llangollen

Address Llangollen Railway Society Ltd, Llangollen Station, Llangollen, Clwyd. Tel. Llangollen 860951

Enquiries to Mr A. Terry, Secretary, at above address

Opening times Daily, 10.00–17.30, including Saturday and Sunday. Steam each Public Holiday and during first week of July each year until Light Railway Order granted

How to get there *By road* A5 Shrewsbury-Holyhead or Wrexham-Ruabon. *By rail* to Ruabon BR, then bus

Facilities Car park, refreshments and souvenir shop

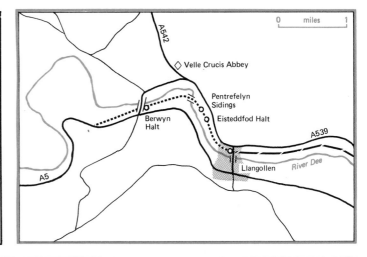

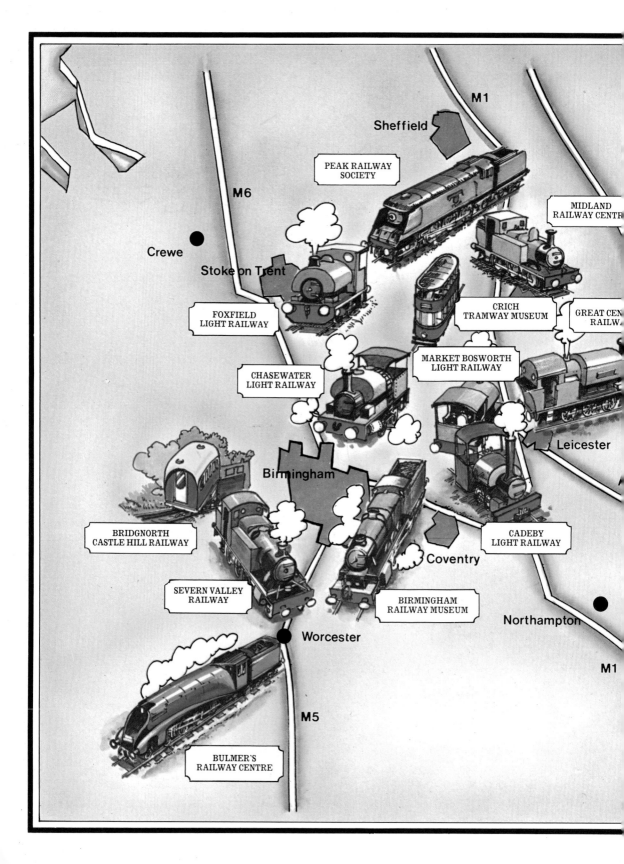

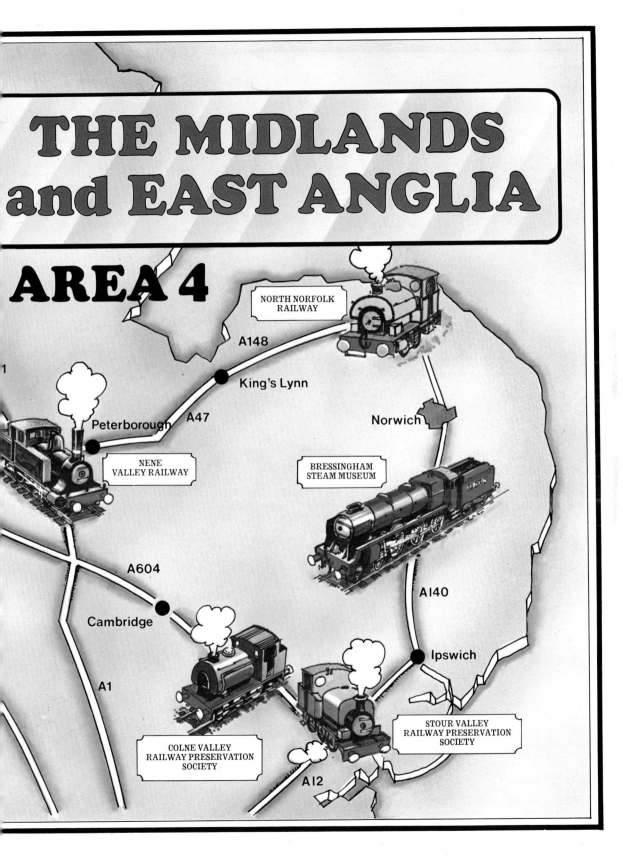

THE MIDLANDS and EAST ANGLIA

AREA 4

NORTH NORFOLK RAILWAY

A148

King's Lynn

Peterborough   A47

Norwich

NENE VALLEY RAILWAY

BRESSINGHAM STEAM MUSEUM

A604

A140

Cambridge

Ipswich

A1

STOUR VALLEY RAILWAY PRESERVATION SOCIETY

COLNE VALLEY RAILWAY PRESERVATION SOCIETY

A12

Bulmer's Railway Centre

Mr Peter Prior, the Managing Director of Bulmer's, the famous Hereford cider-makers, is a dedicated railway enthusiast. In 1967, he was responsible for plans to rescue the much-loved GWR engine *King George V* from a dilapidated shed at Swindon, where she was decaying. In pouring rain, hundreds of railway enthusiasts hauled the *King* on ropes from her lonely dark confines. She was taken to Newport and reboilered, later to become the admired star of a newly created Bulmer's Railway Centre, rail-linked to Hereford station.

Articulate and influential, Mr Prior got strong support for a genuine return to steam movement. In October 1971, hauling a train of Bulmer's Cider Pullmans from Kensington Olympia Station to Swindon, *King George V* became the first locomotive to return to steam upon a British main line since closure of this form of traction in August, 1968.

Also at Bulmer's Centre are a couple of diesel shunters, one made up to look very much like a steam tank engine. They are named *Woodpecker* and *Cider Queen*. Five splendid Pullmans constitute the Bulmer Cider train, one of them fitted up as a cinema and meeting hall. This train goes on runs behind *KGV* (as enthusiasts term the mighty King Class 4–6–0, carrying her bell from ceremonial workings on the Baltimore and Ohio in USA back in 1927), to which are also coupled a rake of ordinary corridor coaches.

Based at Hereford is the 6000 Locomotive Association, taking its title from the official number of *King George V*. Its members act as stewards to the restored locomotive, and they also keep on view at Bulmer's Centre a 0–4–0 saddle tank, the Pullman car *Ruth*, a couple of excellent main line coaches, and some former GWR brake vans. There is enough track at the Centre for the two steam engines to move about and frequent 'open days' are held, some of the most popular and best attended in Britain. Engines from other areas sometimes make visits, and with British Rail's agreement that the main line between Hereford and Crewe via Shrewsbury should be permitted to steam workings, Bulmer's is a preparation base for *KGV* and occasional distinguished visitors.

King George V returns to Bulmer's Railway Centre.

Address Bulmer's Railway Centre, Whitecross Rd, Hereford. Tel. Hereford 6182

Enquiries to H. P. Bulmer Ltd, at above address

Opening times Static displays weekends end March to end September. Steam days last Sunday in each month

How to get there *By road* ½ mile from City centre on A438 to Brecon. *By rail* to Hereford BR

Facilities Car park, refreshments and souvenir shop

Birmingham Railway Museum

Operated by the Standard Gauge Steam
Trust, the Birmingham Railway Museum
is a fairly new title for the motive power
depot known as Tyseley. This site was
built up in the early 1970s and supplies
large engines for authorized steam excursions over British Rail metals. It is at
Tyseley depot in Warwick Road, about 3
miles south-east of the City Centre, not
far from Acock's Green.

Tyseley has 13 steam engines on view,
several of them famous. There is a very
strong Great Western emphasis, the biggest locomotives being three GWR Castles
(*Earl of Mount Edgcumbe, Clun Castle,* and
Thornbury Castle), a fourth – the famous
Pendennis Castle having been sold to
Western Australia. *Albert Hall* is there,
and a 2–6–2 Prairie tank, plus several
typical GWR pannier tanks. The Department of Education and Science loans ex-
LSWR T9 Drummond 4–4–0 which
used to be at Clapham Museum, and the
LMS *Kolhapur* is in the shed, too.

Three fine Pullmans and the London
and North Western Railway Royal Saloon
from 1903 are among the coach exhibits. A
Gresley LNER varnished teak buffet car
and several items of goods stock may be
seen.

When locomotives are in steam, as they
are on many summer Sundays, short rides
are given in the vicinity of the active depot.

ABOVE GWR 4–6–0 No.
7029 *Clun Castle* at
Tyseley.

LEFT No. 7029 *Clun
Castle* inside the workshop
building at Tyseley.

Address Birmingham Railway Museum,
Warwick Rd, Tyseley, Birmingham 11. Tel.
021-707 4696
Enquiries to Above address
Opening times Static displays weekends,
14.00–17.30 for static displays. Closed Bank
Holidays. Steam on summer Sundays
How to get there *By road* A41 Warwick
Rd, 3 miles south-east of city centre. *By rail*
to Tyseley BR
Facilities Car park and well-stocked shop

Severn Valley Railway

Of all the steam railways in Britain, the Severn Valley comes closest to recapturing the experience of making a journey by steam train. It is long enough to enable passengers to settle down and watch the scenery, as well as to thrill to the beat of the engine. It is long enough, too, for trains which omit intermediate stops to achieve speeds reminiscent of a secondary main line in the 1930s.

Based on Bridgnorth, an attractive town astride the River Severn of some 10,000 people, the railway runs for some 13 miles southwards to Bewdley, near Kidderminster. It is a matter of high priority for the railway to extend over the $3\frac{1}{2}$ miles to Kidderminster, where there is an existing British Rail route, but in fact the Severn Valley Railway was formerly part of the

Highley Station on the Severn Valley Railway.

52-mile long Shrewsbury to Worcester secondary line of the Great Western and did not touch Kidderminster. There was a link to that town, however.

The 12.9 miles from Bridgnorth to Bewdley were restored in 1974, but from 1970 (seven years after the BR closure) trains were running from Bridgnorth to Hampton Loade, $4\frac{1}{2}$ miles. The stations on the line (Hampton Loade, Highley, Arley, and Bewdley) all overlook the River Severn at its most scenic. There is a footbridge over the river at Arley, leading to some much-prized angling sites. The old Harbour Inn close to Arley Station attracts interesting customers, especially when the Severn Valley Railway has a filming contract. Recently, David Niven was a frequent visitor, as was Robert Powell during

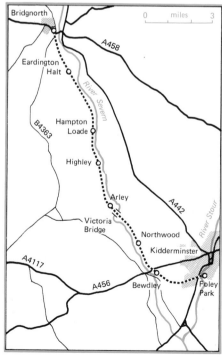

the filming of *The Thirty-Nine Steps*.

The S V R may be unique among pre-served steam railways in having a ghost, one that is seen and reported on with un-canny regularity. The ghost is reckoned to be Fred Jones, former station master of Arley, who swore he would haunt his old station in the event of closure, and it was closed under the Beeching Butchery. He is said to walk about the station at dusk as an old man with a stoop and a mane of white hair, which the licencee of the Harbour Inn declares is a good description of the former customer at the pub.

With plenty of motive power, including two 'Western' type diesel-hydraulic en-gines, and a number of main line coaches plus restaurant and buffet cars, a good service can be maintained when sufficient volunteers are available. Trains run at least three times daily in each direction, and often six times, between mid-July and the end of the first week of September. The timetable is very clear to read and should be consulted before making a special trip. The run takes 43 minutes in a non-stop and 54 minutes in stopping trains.

It is to be hoped that when the line is open to Kidderminster, an all year round service of trains – however skeletal – will be maintained. There is increasing demand from local people and the chance of a school contract. No country bus services follow this route.

Engines and rolling stock are kept at Bridgnorth and Bewdley, which may be viewed free by ticket holders, or at a nominal charge by those not travelling. Excellent souvenir and bookshops are maintained at both these stations. A book on railway nostalgia by the late Sir Gerald Nabarro, the Kidderminster M.P. who was closely associated with the Severn Valley Railway in its formative years, is always on sale.

Recently, the S V R acquired the splen-did post-war British Railways Pacific locomotive No. 70000, *Britannia*. Restora-tion work has been difficult and costly, but the powerful engine should be at work in 1980. There are over 30 steam engines based on the Severn Valley, and various sets of rolling stock, one forming a com-plete ten-coach authentic Great Western train, and another a five-coach L M S R train. Four Castle Class G W R engines exist on the line, plus a 'Hall' and pannier and Prairie tanks, great attractions to the legions of Great Western enthusiasts.

TOP G W R-style train on the Severn Valley Railway.

CENTRE The splendid BR Pacific No. 70000 *Britannia* at Bridgnorth Station.

Address Severn Valley Railway Co Ltd, Railway Station, Bewdley, Worcs, DY12 1BG. Tel. Bewdley 403816 or Bridgnorth 4361

Enquiries to Above address. Timetable available

Opening times Early March to late October, some winter weekends. Daily, mid-July to early September, 10.45–18.00

How to get there *By road* to Bewdley or Bridgnorth. *By rail* to Kidderminster BR

Facilities Car park, refreshments, souvenir and bookshops

Special attractions Special trains for schools. Santa specials, Sunday lunch trains

Discounts For families and groups. Also, unlimited travel on day of purchase for anyone buying a ticket on weekdays in summer. Children half-price

Market Bosworth Light Railway

Chasewater Light Railway

The Market Bosworth Railway has now got itself a run, after lengthy purchase negotiations with British Rail, and the 2¾ miles of standard gauge track between Shackerstone and Market Bosworth is open for steam trains.

It is hoped to extend the line to Shenton, about two more miles in a southerly direction beside the Ashby Canal close to the site of the Battle of Bosworth Field. The 500th anniversary of this Battle is being celebrated in 1985, which will also help the Railway as a tourist carrier.

The tracks are remnants of the former Ashby-de-la-Zouch and Coalville to Nuneaton lines of the old Midland Railway, which junctioned at Shackerstone. Passenger services ceased nearly 20 years ago, so that the reopening of even a small section is a welcome revival in quiet country which has seen little of tourism.

It takes about 12 minutes to run the 2¾ miles from Shackerstone to Market Bosworth, a gentle trip in very rural and authentic country railway settings.

There are eight steam engines and two diesels on the stock, with four passenger carriages. The locomotives are tanks, mostly of industrial origins and fairly new except for a Borrows Well Tank from 1906 called *The King*. The two diesels are also industrial, used for track maintenance and switching duties.

Address Market Bosworth Light Railway, Shackerstone Station, Nr Market Bosworth, Leics.
Enquiries to Timetable available
Opening times Easter Sunday to early October, weekends and Bank Holidays
How to get there *By road* A444, Nuneaton to Burton-on-Trent, turn off for Congerstone. *By rail* to Nuneaton BR and bus
Facilities Car park, refreshments and souvenir shop
Special attractions Museum

This Staffordshire standard gauge line is run by the Railway Preservation Society, having been leased from the National Coal Board in 1965. It runs around the perimeter of the Chasewater and Country Park, which is being expanded. A 2-mile stretch of track has actually been purchased from British Rail, but full services on this are not yet in operation. However, there is enough track (once a tiny part of the historic Cannock Chase and Wolverhampton Railway) to enjoy several minutes behind steam on open days. On part of its route, the Chasewater runs by the edge of an attractive lake and it is not unknown for a water stop to be made, the passengers helping to quench the engine's thirst with buckets.

Eight industrial engines have their home here, plus four diesels. There is a museum with some fine static exhibits including a Midland Railway Royal Saloon from 1912, the Maryport and Carlisle six-wheeled coach (last surviving vehicle from this railway) built in 1879, and a very rare Manchester, Sheffield and Lincolnshire Railway (ancestor of the Great Central) six-wheeled coach from 1890.

Address Chasewater Light Railway, Chasewater Pleasure Park, Nr Brownhills, Walsall, Staffs. Tel. Brownhills 5852
Enquiries to Above address. Timetable available
Opening times All year, weekends from 14.00. Trains run April to October, 2nd and 4th Sundays in the month and Bank Holiday Sundays and Mondays
How to get there *By road* entrance in Pool Rd, Nr Brownhills, off A5 Cannock to Tamworth. 853, 854 bus from Birmingham. *By rail* to Walsall BR
Facilities Car park, refreshments and souvenir shop
Special attractions Museum, and fun park for children
Discounts For families. Children half-price

Cadeby Light Railway

For more than a century, the Church and steam railways have worked in harmony, some of the greatest railway enthusiasts being members of the clergy. The plump and jolly Rector of Cadeby, Reverend 'Teddy' Boston, actually runs a railway as part of his church activities. Around the grounds of his rectory, he has a 2 ft gauge light railway, which, even with extensions, runs scarcely more than $\frac{1}{4}$ mile. It is believed to be the smallest steam-operated narrow gauge railway in the world, and gets plenty of visitors. Cadeby station is at one end of the semi circular track and Sutton Lane at the other.

A fascinating collection of small engines enchants enthusiasts and those who have more than a passing interest in small steam locomotives. There are also miniature diesels and petrol engines in the collection, all housed in the motive power sheds at the Cadeby end. *Pixie,* a o–4–o saddle tank built by Bagnall in 1919 is the favourite of the line, but a German Orenstein and Koppel o–4–o well tank (not unlike the little engines used in India to climb from Neral to Matheran – Bombay's nearest hill

station) runs *Pixie* a close second.

Passenger rides in wooden-sided waggons are available and the ride takes about ten minutes, including a stop at a little halt amid the trees. A collection box for donations to cover fuel and church funds meets the fare, which is left to the discretion of the rider. Anyone in the vicinity should go and see the line, but it is worth telephoning early on the Saturday morning to check that trains will be running.

Address Cadeby Light Railway, Cadeby Rectory, Nr Market Bosworth, Leics. Tel. Market Bosworth 462

Enquiries to Above address

Opening times Trains run April to November, 2nd Saturday in the month

How to get there *By road* A447, 1 mile south of Market Bosworth. Bus to Hinckley. *By rail* to Hinckley BR (frequent service from Nuneaton BR)

Facilities Car park and refreshments

Special attractions Steam museum at Cadeby end of the line. Model railway layout based on a Great Western theme

The favourite at Cadeby: Bagnall o–4–o saddle tank *Pixie.*

Midland Railway Centre

With a tremendous collection of genuine Midland locomotives and rolling stock, this Steam Centre will be one of the leading preservation groups in Britain once it achieves its operating mileage. The project is to preserve the much revered memory of the Midland Railway and the early years of the London, Midland and Scottish (up to 1930 this was still dominated by Midland practice).

The collection is on view at Butterley, not far from Derby. About 15 engines include a vintage 2–4–0 express engine built in 1866 and which the LMS kept running on normal service (but by then on secondary branch lines) until 1947. There are four of the popular 'Jinty' 0–6–0 tanks, a splendid 4F heavy 0–6–0 goods engine, the graceful single dfiver by Johnson, No. 673, a 4–2–2 built in 1890 and one of the last express single drivers kept in service (until 1922), the magnificent Stanier Pacific *Princess Margaret Rose,* and a very new (for steam) standard 4–6–0, a Caprotti Black Five from 1956. Some smaller industrial engines are there as well.

The centre has a large number of real Midland carriages, including clerestories from early Edwardian days, together with vans and goods trucks. Perhaps the most remarkable exhibit is the body of a Midland Pullman from 1874, one of several imported from the United States, ready for the Midland's Anglo-Scottish services over the Settle and Carlisle line.

It is intended that the main museum will be moved to Swanwick when a running line of reasonable length is achieved. The idea is to have a double track line between Asher Lane, Ripley, and Swanwick Colliery Junction. A single line will run on to Pye Bridge, making 3¼ miles of operating length. Butterley Engineering, the present 'Midland hosts' already lease the stretch from Swanwick to near Pye Bridge from British Rail. There are also plans to run a 3ft gauge line in North Derbyshire.

These projects seem ambitious and as all preservation lines are perennially short of hard cash, it may take some time before the schemes reach fruition. But with such a

Ex-LMS 3F 16440 waiting to depart from Butterley Station.

mass of appropriate equipment, and a great deal of goodwill and nostalgia for the Midland Railway, the whole thing could be working by the mid 1980s.

Address Midland Railway Trust Ltd, Butterley Station, Nr Ripley, Derbys. Tel. Ripley 44920

Enquiries to Above address

Opening times Every Saturday and Sunday, last week-end in March to end October, 10.00–18.00. Steam every Bank Holiday

How to get there *By road* A61, Derby to Chesterfield, 1½ miles north of Ripley. *By rail* to BR Alfreton and Mansfield Parkway, then bus

Facilities Free car park, refreshments and souvenir shop

Discounts for families

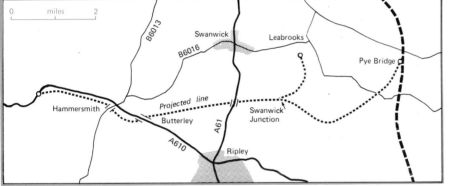

ABOVE Locomotive 6203 *Princess Margaret Rose* at Butterley Station.

BOTTOM LEFT Stanton 24 0–4–0 crane tank at work in Butterley Station goods yard.

BELOW Ex-Midland Railway 158A Kirtley, built in 1866.

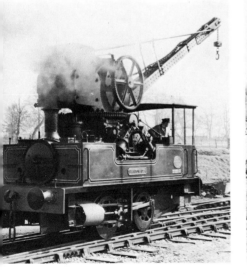

Great Central Railway

Properly called the Main Line Steam Trust, the 'Great Central' is a reopened stretch of standard gauge line on the former Great Central's route from Leicester to Nottingham. The Trust is a company limited by guarantee and registered as a charity. However, as Great Central Railway Company (1976) Ltd, the organisation went public to raise sufficient funds to buy the track between Loughborough Central Station and Rothley, a distance of exactly 5 miles. This was the last surviving section of the main line of the Great Central built from Sheffield to London (Marylebone) via Nottingham, Leicester and Rugby in 1898–99. It was the last main line to be built in Britain and the first to employ relatively modern construction methods, such as steam shovels and battery electric drills. It was a costly and optimistic project, which never paid off, but performed wonderful work and became extremely popular in Edwardian England, with the fastest route to Sheffield from 1905 to 1914. It beat the competition (Midland Railway) with speed and comfort, but failed to show a clear profit.

The original idea was to restore a double-track main line in the heart of the Midland 'Shire' country, at least 8 miles long, to re-create the effect of main line steam operations in the 1930s and 1940s. The sheer cost has defeated the enthusiasts, who have no exceptional scenic attractions to offer and would have needed to rely wholly on railway enthusiasts and nostalgia. The prospect of good film contracts was there, but before anything solid could result in this direction, the line had to be singled to raise money and so the Great Central no longer looks like a great main line of the past.

Hopes of reaching Birstall, 8 miles south of Loughborough, seem to have faded, but trains are run between Loughborough and Rothley via a sturdy, spacious typical Great Central wayside station at Quorn and Woodhouse. There is enough left to give the flavour of the old Great Central, helped by the excellent condition of Loughborough Central Station, its waiting room and museums, and the temporary possession of former GCR 4–4–0 *Butler Henderson,* a Director class belonging to the National Collection.

In all, the railway has twenty steam engines, two diesels, and eight coaches. The locomotives are widely representative of all companies, including a Great Western Hall class, and a Southern Railway Bulleid Pacific. One oddity is a Norwegian 2–6–0, *King Haakon VII,* acquired from the Norwegian State Railways. There are some large and small industrial tank engines, sometimes used in pairs on relatively modern British Rail rolling stock. Hopes are high that the 4–6–2 *Duke of Gloucester,* a 1954 'one-off' experimental loco, might run on the GCR. It awaits complete restoration at Loughborough under its own Trust.

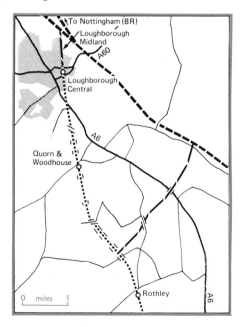

Bridgnorth Castle Hill Railway

A great deal of hard work by enthusiastic volunteers has led to construction of a massive 12,500 sq ft locomotive and maintenance shed at Loughborough where restoration work continues. The collection of main line engines alone makes a visit to the railway worthwhile.

The Great Central produces its own magazine, a glossy quarterly called 'Main Line'. Subscriptions not only to this but to ordinary shares are eagerly sought to enable operations to continue and to expand.

The run itself is through rural hunting country, fairly level but with a climb out of Rothley in the northerly direction. The largest engineering work is the handsome Swithland Viaduct, crossing a reservoir. The Great Central possesses a couple of Gresley buffet cars and a bar-coach enabling it to offer a round trip dining car excursion for special occasions, while on other trains it serves draught beer during the journey. Limited by Light Railway Order to low speeds, it is not usually possible for this 'Main Line' to run at more than 30 miles an hour and the journey to Rothley with one stop on the way takes some 20 minutes. The round trip may be reckoned as one hour but visitors usually spend a good deal of time seeing the attractions at Loughborough Central.

Address Great Central Railway (Main Line Steam Trust Ltd), Great Central Rd, Loughborough, Leics. Tel. Loughborough 216433

Enquiries to Above address. Timetable available

Opening times Weekends and Bank Holidays, Wednesdays and Thursdays in July and August

How to get there *By road* A6 to Loughborough, between Leicester and Derby or M1. *By rail* to Loughborough BR

Facilities Car park, refreshments and souvenir shop

Linking Lower Town with Upper Town in this pleasant community astride the River Severn is a funicular railway. Equipped with two cars, it raises passengers up 201 ft with a gradient of 4 in 7, making it the longest and steepest inland cliff railway in Great Britain.

Originally it was worked by hydraulic power, but a switch to electricity and more modern passenger cars was made in the late 1930s. The ride takes less than a minute, and a return ticket saves both time and money compared to taking a bus or driving from Lower Town to the offices, shops and historic buildings of Upper Bridgnorth.

Visitors to the Severn Valley Railway, whose terminus is less than half a mile from the Lower Town entrance to the Cliff Railway, should experience this dramatic hill climb. The Cliff Railway works every day except Christmas and Boxing Day.

Bridgnorth Castle Hill Railway.

Peak Railway Society

This is the most ambitious project of all involved in railway preservation, planning as it does to restore the former Midland main line between Matlock and Buxton, closed in 1968. It will involve about twenty miles of main line, over spectacular viaducts which are fortunately still standing and through five tunnels.

Formed in 1975, the Society so far has managed to lease Matlock station buildings and the adjoining goods yard, while planning permission has been obtained to develop the site of Buxton Midland station as a restoration and working steam centre. The Derbyshire County Council has approved in principle the railway land being used again for railway purposes, through the most beautiful part of the Peak District.

Several steam engines have been reserved at Barry scrapyard, with a Southern Region West Country Pacific *Hartland* now moved and in store at Derby. No trains run as yet although an active publicity campaign with car stickers gives the

RIGHT Former Booking Hall at Matlock Station, now fully restored and in use as a railway shop.

BELOW A spectacular viaduct on the former Midland main line.

impression that something is soon to happen. It would seem to be a project whose completion is at least ten years in the future.

British Rail diesel units maintain a service from Derby to Matlock, serving on the way Matlock Bath where a large model railway system with a Midland 'Peak' theme may be visited.

Address Peak Railway Society Ltd, Matlock Bath Station, Matlock

How to get there *By road* A6 Matlock to Belper. *By rail* to Matlock Bath BR

Facilities Refreshments, souvenir shop at Matlock

Crich Tramway Museum

Built in a vast Derbyshire quarry more than a thousand feet up in the southern part of the Peak District, Crich is more than just a very interesting collection of tramcars. It offers a delightful scenic tramway ride, roughly following the track of a mineral railway built by the famous George Stephenson.

The Tramway Museum was set up in 1959, two years after the quarry closed down and the railway stopped working. Tramcars preserved by small groups soon made their way to Crich, which rapidly became the national home for these vehicles. Now there are some 40 trams based in the big sheds, ranging from an Oporto car of 1873 to a Leeds tram from 1953, the last urban tram to have been built for use in a British city. It is inevitable, in view of the fact that Leeds, Sheffield, and Glasgow kept their big double-decker trams in action so much longer than other places, that there are more representatives of them at Crich.

About ten cars are at present operational, and these come out of the sheds to give rides. Another eight or ten vehicles are works machines, track-grinders or cable-layers from various extinct tramway systems, and there is also an enclosed steam tram. Sturdy old Edwardian open-top trams are the favourites for fine weather rides.

Only Blackpool continues to have a municipal tramway system in mainland Britain, but at the height of the tram's success, in the mid 1920s, almost every city and big town had them, owning some 14,000 vehicles. Modern trams are obviously the city transport of the future, as has been proved in Western and Central Europe and in several American cities. Newcastle-on-Tyne will see the return of the tram by 1981, in ultra-modern 'Metro' form.

The run at Crich lasts about 12 minutes, with a midway stop where passengers may change trams. There is a dramatic view to

the left of the line over the Peak District, while to the right, high above the quarry cliffs, is the tower monument to the Sherwood Foresters who died in the two World Wars. One return trip by tram is included in the admission charge to Crich. On Bank Holidays big tram extravaganzas are staged.

Part of Crich's unique collection of trams.

Address Tramway Museum Society, Crich, Nr Ambergate, Derby, DE4 5DP. Tel. 2562
Enquiries to Above address
Opening times Weekends, April to October, 11.30–19.30, Mid-week, June, July, August, 10.00–17.00
How to get there By road B5035, off A6 Matlock to Belper. Frequent Trent and Midland bus. By rail to Whatstandwell Matlock BR (but no Sunday service)
Facilities Free car park, refreshments, souvenir and book shop

99

Stour Valley Railway Preservation Society

The Stour Valley is an ambitious East Anglian Society, not unlike that of North Norfolk, which has great potential yet is at present unable to get very far. It is based at Chappel and Wakes Colne Station in Essex, on the former Colchester to Cambridge line, the last in Britain to have 2–4–0 locomotives hauling over a 40-mile stretch (they were not finally withdrawn until 1957).

Given the new spirit of co-operation emanating from top management of British Rail, the Stour Valley line could go forward to great success. Meanwhile it occupies itself with steam days at its restored rural station, hoping one day either to take over the BR operated Marks Tey to Sudbury line or to put services back on the Sudbury to Long Melford section.

There is to some extent a Great Eastern atmosphere about the stock at Chappel and Wakes Colne, with an N7 class 0–6–2 tank from Great Eastern days, and a couple of four-wheelers from earlier GER days. A fairly modern 2–6–4 BR standard tank is there, and several industrial tanks. In all there are eight steam engines, two diesels, and eleven carriages.

Address Stour Valley Railway Preservation Society, Chappel and Wakes Colne Station, Chappel, Colchester, Essex. Tel. Earls Colne 2571

Enquiries to Publicity Officer, at above address. Open day details available

Opening times Every weekend, 11.00–18.00. Steam days – first Sunday of month, March to November, and Bank Holidays

How to get there By road off A604 Colchester to Haverhill. By rail to Chappel and Wakes Colne BR via Marks Tey

Facilities Car park, refreshments, souvenir shop and extensive bookshop

Discounts For groups of 20 or more, if booked in advance. Children half-price

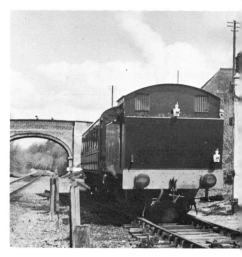

TOP 0–6–0 saddle tank, *Penn Green*.

CENTRE Ex-GER 0–6–2 tank No. 999 N7 class, built in 1924.

BOTTOM Signals and signal box at Chappel North.

Foxfield Light Railway

This is *the* preserved railway for lovers of industrial tank engines, for the Foxfield musters no less than 14 of them, including the largest and best collection of Bagnalls to be found anywhere. It also offers the visitor (who must become a temporary member for a day to use the facilities) a chance to see a deeply rural branch working coupled with former colliery activity.

The railway was laid in 1893 to link Foxfield Colliery in Staffordshire with the North Staffordshire Railway (the old 'Knotty') at Blythe Bridge, a station on that railway's Uttoxeter to Stoke-on-Trent line. Blythe Bridge is still an active BR station on the Derby–Uttoxeter-Stoke route.

Closed more than a decade ago, the colliery now belongs to Tean Minerals Ltd, owners of the Foxfield Railway, who permit the Railway Society to operate steam trains over its $3\frac{1}{2}$ miles of track. The line is very interesting, with gradients on its standard gauge as steep as 1 in 20 (unheard of on normal passenger-carrying lines) and sharp curves. The summit of the route exceeds 700ft, where good views are obtained. For part of the run the line passes through dense woodlands, and there is a sight of stately 17th century Stansmore Hall. The steam ride takes some 22 minutes each way, with a stop at Dilhorne Park where picnic facilities are provided.

Services operate from the Foxfield end only, as no connection is made with the British Rail line to Blythe Bridge, although in the more favourable climate of co-operation existing today, this may eventually come.

In addition to the fleet of colliery and industrial tank engines, admirably suited to such a line, there are two diesels, and five operating coaches, three of them standard BR Mark One's. Static equipment on view includes four ex-LMS bogie scenery vans, one converted to provide refreshments, and a Smith Rodley steam crane.

Address Foxfield Light Railway, Foxfield Colliery, Dilhorne, Blythe Bridge, Nr Stoke-on-Trent, Staffs.

Enquiries to The Secretary, Foxfield Light Railway Society Ltd., 25 Drubbery Lane, Dresden, Stoke-on-Trent, Staffs. Tel. Stoke-on-Trent 313920

Opening times Sundays and Bank Holidays, April to September, 13.30–18.00

How to get there *By road* between A50 and A52, turn left at Blythe Bridge. *By rail* to Blythe Bridge BR, then bus

Facilities Car park, refreshments, picnic area and souvenir shop

Special attractions 'Wine and dine specials' on certain Saturdays

Discounts On application. Children half-price

Nene Valley Railway

Here is something unique so far as British preserved lines are concerned. It has a strong Scandinavian flavour, reminiscent of train rides in Denmark or Sweden in the early 1950s, or even pre-war, and somehow enhanced by the pastoral and fairly level scenery along the water meadows of the Nene.

The Nene Valley Railway is a single track section, just over 6 miles long, surviving from the 1845 branch line built by the London and North Western Railway from Rugby and Northampton to Peterborough. In those days the Cathedral City of the Fens had not yet been linked by the famous main line of the Great Northern out of King's Cross. Passengers who wanted to travel to Peterborough either did so by Eastern Counties out of Liverpool Street or from Euston via Northampton, changing on to the Nene Valley.

Yarwell Junction, a former track bifurcation amid the meadows, is the present western limit of track. Of the lines to Rugby and Northampton there are only overgrown remains. Just over half a mile eastwards from Yarwell Junction lies the handsome station of Wansford, headquarters of the Nene Valley Railway. The

route continues beside – and across – the Nene river for $5\frac{1}{2}$ rural miles to Orton Mere, a newly built station quite close to Peterborough. In fact, a freight line still in use continues on and round a corner to junction with the British Rail main line from King's Cross into Peterborough's newly rebuilt station. An extension over this line is many years ahead but a short push and pull from Wansford to Yarwell is expected to start soon.

There were two intermediate stations, one at Castor, closed some 30 years ago but intended to be rebuilt in future years, and one at Ferry Meadows, built up now as a halt. Orton station is dismantled and its site transferred eastwards to Orton Mere, the terminus of passenger trips.

The Peterborough Railway Society was created in 1972 out of various enthusiast organisations which had bought and preserved engines. Designated a New Town, Peterborough was expanding and its Development Corporation worked with the Railway Society to acquire and reopen the Nene Valley line. In fact, the railway runs on land owned by the Corporation.

A tremendous amount of work had to be put in at the beginning to restore the line to anything like working order. Chickens had been kept in the lovely old London and North Western Railway signal box at Wansford, now in pristine condition. This has 60 levers and is probably the largest preserved box in the country. Wansford had an engine shed and sidings built, pointwork was put in at the new Orton Mere, and coal and water facilities were brought back to the line. Engines were acquired, also rolling stock.

When trains first started running, it was just another preserved British type branch line, pleasant and nostalgic, serving an area starved of steam for many years, but not very different to enthusiasts' railways in other parts of the country. Then someone made an important decision to increase the loading gauge to accommodate

Danish State Railways 0–6–0 tank No. 656 on the Nene Valley Railway.

larger Continental locomotives and rolling stock, which only needed a low bridge (a road overhead) to be demolished and the Wansford platform edges to be set back. Once this was done, the 'Berne' gauge was on hand. The spectacle of period Continental trains could be observed in England, running with British ones. That is why the distance from Wansford to Orton Mere is now shown as 8.2kms.

A heavy Swedish 2–6–4 tank built by Nohab in 1953 was obtained. Also a delightful little Danish 0–6–0 tank engine, one of a batch built as recently as 1949 yet designed in Victorian times, used for shunting heavy trains on and off ferries at Nyborg. A Swedish 2–6–2 tank of 1914 built at Motala joined the Nene Valley, and so did a De Glehn 4–6–0 from Calais Shed, a famous Nord type express engine from 1911 (although this example was actually built by Henschel in Germany). A rake of red-painted Danish corridor coaches was obtained, at only £500 per coach. Newest addition to the rolling stock is a genuine Wagon-Restaurant, built in 1927 by the Wagons-Lits Company. This was obtained with the aid of Thomas Cook, the travel company so long associated with Wagons-Lits, which has its head offices at Thorpe Wood, Peterborough, within sight of the Nene Valley line.

There are several British engines, big ones such as the modern 'Black Five' of 1954, named *City of Peterborough*, the Southern streamlined Bulleid Pacific No. 34081 *92 Squadron* of the Battle of Britain Class, and a whole string of industrial tank engines. Several Southern coaches, from electric stock, and a Pullman named *Bertha*, are available to make up British trains.

But the train I rode in June 1979 was purely Scandinavian, the red Danish coaches plus the blue and gold Wagon-Restaurant, hauled by *Tinkerbelle*, the strong little Danish tank. It was like a ride on a Copenhagen-Hamburg express while being pulled towards the 'Bird's Flight' ferry at Rodby.

This Continental aspect has paid off in film-making and in an appeal to foreign visitors. The railway scenes for BBC TV's *Secret Army* series were shot on the Nene Valley. Producers now know they do not have to go on location abroad for French, Swedish, Danish or Norwegian train scenes. There is even a Norwegian State Railways suburban carriage available.

Swedish State Railways 2–6–4 tank No. 1928, now owned by the Nene Valley Railway.

Address Nene Valley Railway, Wansford Station, Stibbington, Peterborough, Northants. Tel. Stamford 782854

Enquiries to The General Manager, at above address. Timetable available

Opening times April to October, Sundays, 11.00–18.00, Saturdays and mid-week, 12.00–16.00

How to get there *By road* Just off A1, 1 mile south of junction with A47. *By rail* to Peterborough BR

Facilities Free car park, refreshments, picnic areas and souvenir shop at Wansford

Special attractions 'Santa specials' with sherry and mince pies, at weekends in December. Sunday lunches in the Wagon Restaurant

Discounts For families and groups. Children and OAPs half-price

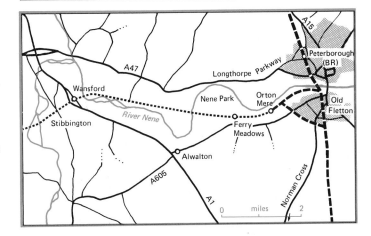

Bressingham Steam Museum

At Bressingham Hall, two miles from the town of Diss in Norfolk, is a considerable acreage of beautiful gardens and nurseries. The owner, Mr Alan Bloom, loves flowers and railways. It is fortunate for all railway enthusiasts that he does so, for he has gathered a fine collection of steam engines and has saved many from extinction.

In a special display building are housed several engines from the official British Rail Collection, and some which have been brought in from Butlins Holiday Camps. When Sir William Butlin was actively running his camps he saved various steam locomotives, large and small. He now lives in Jersey and others not particularly interested in steam nostalgia run the business. Credit, though, must go to Butlins in the 1967–72 era because many engines including *Royal Scot* would have gone to the torch without Sir William.

They now have a better home and are well cared for. There is $\frac{1}{4}$ mile of standard gauge track on which some of these en-gines are steamed and moved on demonstrations which delight children in particular. There is $\frac{1}{2}$ mile of $9\frac{1}{2}$ in gauge track for miniature engines to give rides around the Park. In addition, a Nursery Railway 2 miles long is laid to the Festiniog Gauge (1 ft $11\frac{1}{2}$ in), and another, termed 'Waveney Valley Railway', of $2\frac{1}{2}$ miles on 15 in (Romney, Hythe and Dymchurch) gauge. So, there are plenty of rides to choose from and engines to enjoy on a full steam day at Bressingham, while non-railway people can appreciate the glorious flowers or the woodlands. A recent controversy about footplate rides at Bressingham, which were banned by a BR Inspector, has now been resolved and the footplates of engines with steam up can again be visited.

In all there are 24 steam engines, with ex-LMS Pacific *Duchess of Sutherland* occupying pride of place alongside BR standard Pacific *Oliver Cromwell* and the famous *Royal Scot* No. 6100. Many other famous engines are there to be

No. 6100, the famous *Royal Scot*, as rebuilt with taper boiler.

Colne Valley Railway Preservation Society

admired including a big 'Kriegslok' built in Germany and used by the Norwegian State Railways and a French 1–4–1 R built in America in 1945.

On the 15 in gauge, Mr Bloom managed to buy a splendid pair of twins from Dusseldorf where they had been in store, the Krupp Pacifics *Rosenkavalier* and *Mannertreu*, built in 1937. On the virtually 2 ft gauge line, there is an eagerly sought-after Orenstein and Koppel engine, a 0–4–0 well tank named *Eigiau* from 1912, plus a few ubiquitous Dinorwic or other Welsh slate quarries tanks. One handsome little Pacific, called *Princess*, built in 1947 serves the 9½ in gauge railway.

There is one active diesel, mainly for works purposes, at Bressingham, and four carriages, one an eastern counties four-wheeler of 1850, but no less than 19 open toast-racks for rides on the 15 in gauge. A Beyer Peacock 0–4–0 + 0–4–0 Garrett may be seen, if not on loan to the National Museum at York. It is the only surviving standard gauge UK Garret.

Bressingham is fully equipped with all the facilities visitors to railway centres have come to expect. There is also a new exhibition hall with 7,000 square ft of space for road steam engines, cased exhibits, and a OO gauge model layout. A steam organ and steam roundabout entertain children.

Address Bressingham Steam Museum and Gardens, Nr Diss, Norfolk, IP22 2AB. Tel. Bressingham 386

Enquiries to Above address. Timetable available

Opening times Easter, then every Sunday from early May to end September, Thursdays late May to early September, every Wednesday afternoon in August

Facilities Free car park, refreshments and souvenir shop

Special attractions Museum, steam organ and steam roundabout

How to get there *By road* A1066 2 miles west of Diss. *By rail* to Diss BR

On the same former Great Eastern cross-country route as the Stour Valley Preservation Society is the Colne Valley Preservation Society, based at Castle Hedingham, but operated separately. So far it has a static display of six steam engines, and a museum. There are plans to build a short standard gauge line on the track bed of the Colne Valley and Halstead line, for the society's industrial tank engines.

The Colne Valley Society is supported by the Gravesend Railway Enthusiasts Society, which steams a small Hawthorn Leslie 0–4–0 saddle tank on steam days.

Address Colne Valley Railway Preservation Society, Castle Hedingham Station, Nr Halstead, Essex. Tel. Hedingham 61174

Enquiries to Above address

Opening times Daily. Steam days at Bank Holiday weekends

How to get there *By road* A604, ½ mile north of Castle Hedingham. *By rail* to Braintree BR

Facilities Car park, refreshments and souvenir shop

Special attractions Museum

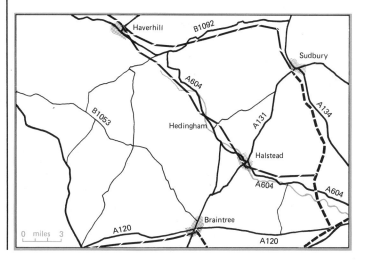

North Norfolk Railway

The first preservation group to appeal for public support by way of shares on the Stock Market, the North Norfolk line has still a long way to go to reach the big league of steam operations for pleasure. Fifteen years of hard work and a good deal of money has so far continued to provide the line with a 3-mile run from Sheringham to Weybourne. Their star attraction, the last surviving B12 4–6–0 of Great Eastern origin, needs many thousands of pounds spent on it before it steams over the stiff gradients to Weybourne again.

The route is a tiny part of the old Midland and Great Northern Joint Railway, which at one time ran from Little Bytham and Peterborough to King's Lynn, Cromer, Norwich and Yarmouth, passing through miles of lonely country. The section between Sheringham (M&GN) and Melton Constable, 13 miles along the North Norfolk coast, was scenically the best on its long run, as the Melton Constable to Cromer branch served cliff-top villages and high heathland. The area currently served is designated as being of outstanding natural beauty.

There is still some hope that a 3½-mile extension to Holt across Kelling Heath might be achieved. But the railway, which is strongly supported by the M&GN Joint Railway Society, needs more revenue and more riders. It is not remote in the same way as North Yorkshire Moors Railway, although there are not yet sufficient local people as steady supporters. But for anyone holidaying at Cromer, Sheringham, or anywhere in Norfolk as far as The Wash, a ride to Weybourne is a must. It takes about 15 minutes, these days usually behind an industrial tank, as both Great Eastern engines (they have a 0–6–0 of the once ubiquitous J15 class) are awaiting heavy repairs. But near miracles can occur and may have occurred between writing these words and appearance in print.

The line steams to a timetable that is complicated and should be checked. There are 10 steam engines, 5 diesels, 19 passenger coaches, (some of them close-coupled ex-GER suburban stock), a museum, a good shop, a café, and ample car parking. This could yet become one of the great preserved lines, but another 10 years, and a lot of sympathetic help, is still needed. Fees for film-making are a useful source of revenue. The North Norfolk was used for sequences of BBC TV's *Dad's Army*.

Ex-GER 0–6–0 No. 564 passes Sheringham Golf Course.

Address North Norfolk Railway Co, The Station, Sheringham, Norfolk, NR26 8RA. Tel. Sheringham 822045

Enquiries to Above address. Timetable available

Opening times Sheringham base – daily, Easter to October, otherwise weekends, 10.00–17.00. Steam, April to September, weekends Easter to October (see timetable for details)

How to get there *By road* Near Sheringham town centre, adjacent to A149 coast road. *By rail* to Sheringham BR

Facilities Car park, refreshments and souvenir shop

Discounts For groups of 10 or more, if booked in advance. Children half-price

LEFT Lunches on the Brighton Belle Pullman. On the left No. 564.

CENTRE Peckett 0–6–0 saddle tank No. 5 *John D. Hammer* pulls away from Sheringham with a train for Weybourne.

BOTTOM 0–6–0 saddle tank *Colwyn* heads a Weybourne train out of Sheringham.

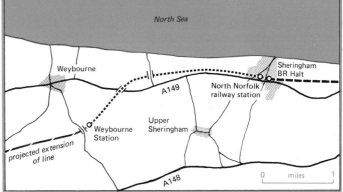

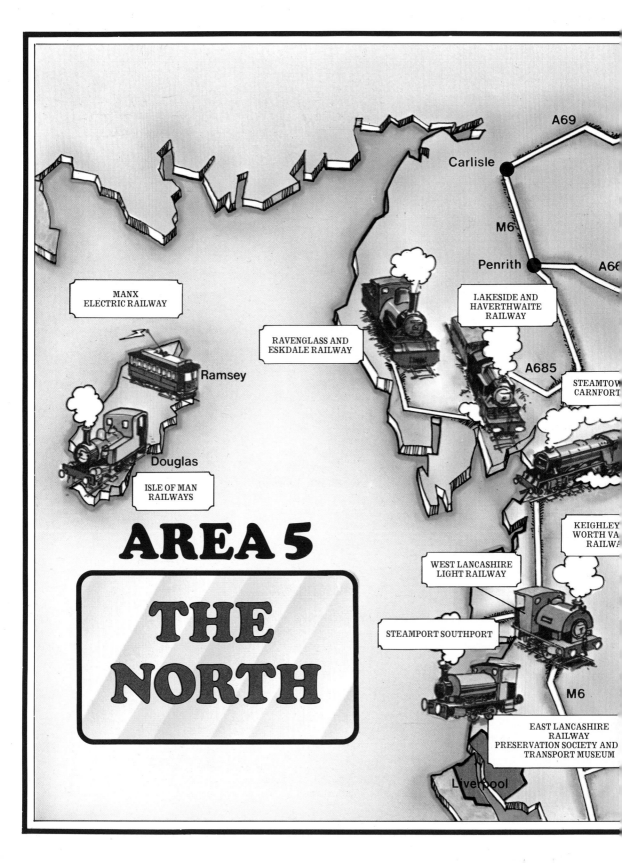

MANX
ELECTRIC RAILWAY

Ramsey

ISLE OF MAN
RAILWAYS

Douglas

RAVENGLASS AND
ESKDALE RAILWAY

Carlisle

A69

M6

Penrith

A66

LAKESIDE AND
HAVERTHWAITE
RAILWAY

A685

STEAMTOW
CARNFORT

KEIGHLEY
WORTH VA
RAILWA

WEST LANCASHIRE
LIGHT RAILWAY

STEAMPORT SOUTHPORT

M6

EAST LANCASHIRE
RAILWAY
PRESERVATION SOCIETY AND
TRANSPORT MUSEUM

Liverpool

AREA 5

THE NORTH

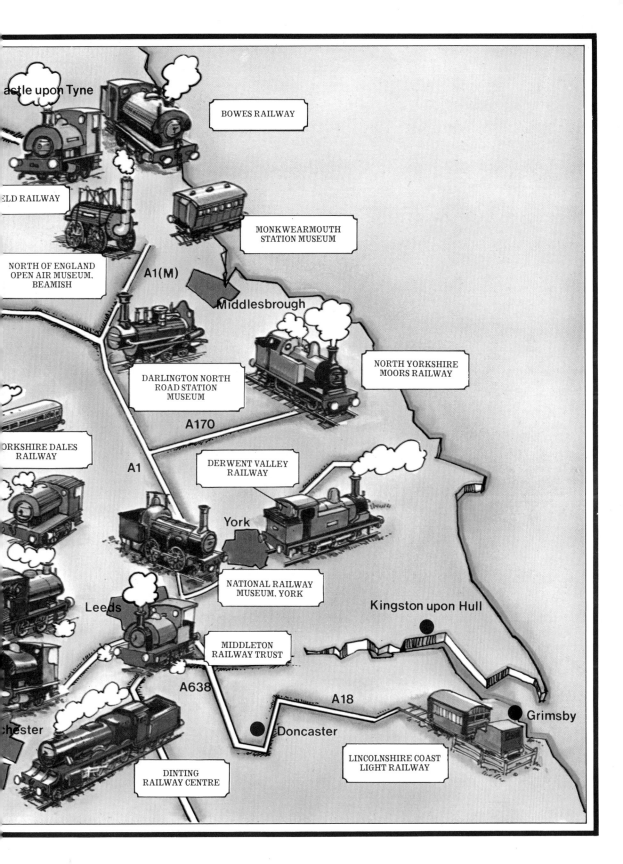

Dinting Railway Centre

Part of Dinting Lane, about a mile from the busy station of Glossop, houses a collection of working and static steam engines. It is almost within the outer surburbs of Manchester, yet close by rear the high bleak hills of the North Peak.

Once an important depot of the old Great Central Railway, Dinting's 10-acre site is really for the knowledgeable rail fan or the family touring nearby who might like to learn a bit more about the glories of steam.

Normally there are twelve engines on site, plus two diesels. There are no runs, but from time to time, Dinting supplies an engine for a steam special, and then there is hustle and bustle with some fine sights to see. Normally, one or more engines are steamed for visitors every Sunday between early March and the end of October. Steaming is also staged on all Bank Holiday weekends except Christmas.

Pride of the collection is an ex-LMS 'Royal Scot', *Scots Guardsman*, largely restored on site. Another ex-LMS engine is the graceful 'Jubilee' *Bahamas*, which goes away at the head of specials to Sheffield from time to time. A second 'Jubilee', *Leander*, is cleared for running BR specials and the former Southern Railway Schools

class engine *Cheltenham*, a 4–4–0, should also be heading specials shortly. A genuine former Great Central Railway loco lives at Dinting; she is a 2–8–0 freight engine of the O4 class built in 1911. Several industrial tank engines are to be seen about the place and there is an exhibition hall 200ft long. Rolling stock is confined to a coach and one or two waggons.

The Centre, a registered charity, came to life when the Bahamas Railway Society was formed in 1967 with the object of restoring the Jubilee class engine and stabling her at a convenient location. *Bahamas* was the first of the 12 engines to come to Dinting.

Address Dinting Railway Centre, Dinting Lane, Glossop, Derbys. Tel. Glossop 5596

Enquiries to Above address

Opening times Steaming on Sundays early March to end October and Bank Holiday weekends, except Christmas

How to get there *By road* A57 Manchester, 1 mile from Glossop. Manchester buses Nos 236 or 125. *By rail* to Dinting BR

Facilities Free car park, refreshments, picnic area and souvenir shop

Discounts Reduced rate for children

0–6–0 saddle tank No. 150
Warrington, built in 1944.

ABOVE Ex-LNWR No. 1054 at Dinting Railway Centre.

LEFT Ex-LMS 'Royal Scot' *Scots Guardsman* was largely restored on site at Dinting.

Lincolnshire Coast Light Railway

East Lancashire
Railway Preservation Society and Bury Transport Museum

Situated at Humberstone, near Grimsby in Lincolnshire, this little narrow gauge railway (1ft 11½in, similar to that of the famous Festiniog) was built new in 1960. Six years later it was re-aligned and extended, and now runs a distance of one mile. It is purely a pleasure line to serve holidaymakers at Cleethorpes a couple of miles away, and will appeal to families having an outing rather than to the dedicated enthusiast.

There are five Simplex diesels working on the line which is open daily from late May to mid-October, but at weekends steam haulage is more or less guaranteed. The line has two steam locomotives, one a Peckett 0–6–0 saddle tank from 1903 and the other a Hunslet 0–4–0 saddle tank from 1899, obtained from the Penrhyn Castle Museum. The journey takes about 12 minutes each way with open carriages in fair weather and closed saloons in wet or chilly conditions.

Groups of enthusiasts have gathered some steam locomotives and rolling stock of standard gauge for eventual use on a section of preserved line in the general area of Bury. So far, no running track has been acquired but the Preservation Society has developed the East Lancashire Goods Depot at Bury and named it Bury Transport Museum.

In the depot are six steam engines, two diesels, two carriages, and various wagons, while the Museum contains vintage cars, buses, a steam roller and a fire engine. The engines are all sturdy former industrial tanks, an ex-Manchester Ship Canal locomotive being of particular interest. Built in 1903 by Hudswell Clarke, it is a 0–6–0 tank named *Gothenburg*. Among the items of rolling stock are a hand crane from the Midland Railway (built in 1880) and a Lancashire and Yorkshire Railway four-wheeled goods van. The Society owns a couple of British Rail coaches from 1956, which it is hoped will eventually provide comfortable passenger accommodation when a stretch of track becomes available for runs.

Address Lincolnshire Coast Light Railway, North Sea Lane, Humberston, Grimsby, Humberside

Enquiries to General Manager, at above address

Opening times Easter, Spring Bank Holiday week, mid-July to mid-September. Steam at weekends

How to get there *By road* A16, A18 and A46. Grimsby-Cleethorpes Transport buses. *By rail* to Cleethorpes or Grimsby BR, then bus

Facilities Car park, refreshments and souvenir shop

Address East Lancashire Railway Preservation Society, Bury Transport Museum, Castlecroft Rd, Bury, Lancs, BL9 0LN. Tel. 061-764 7790

Enquiries to Above address

Opening times Weekends (except Christmas) from 11.00. Steam last Sunday of every month from March to September, also Bank Holidays

How to get there *By road* A56, 8 miles north of Manchester. *By rail* to Bury BR

Facilities Car park. Refreshments and souvenir shop on steam days

Special attractions Model railway

Steamport Southport

On a much smaller scale than Steamtown at Carnforth, this is a locomotive and transport society catering for Merseyside and is an attraction. Steamport occupies the site of the former Southport Derby Road Shed of British Rail steam days, and is a limited company with a good stock of ten steam engines and two passenger carriages.

There are four tracks leading into the depot, and steaming plus a very limited movement is possible. No actual run is envisaged, but steamings take place. The depot is open as a museum throughout the year.

Biggest of the preserved engines is a Stanier Black Five, No. 44806 *Magpie*, once a frequenter of the Merseyside tracks. A relatively modern British Rail Class 4 2–6–0 dates from 1957. Several industrial tank engines with a Merseyside flavour are based here, plus a diesel crane and some LMS goods wagons. The two passenger coaches are fairly modern bogies, one of LMS origin, the other a BR Mark 1 (which was based on the LMS style).

The 'Silver Belle' train, on 2ft gauge, which at one time operated on Southport Pier with its engine and four coaches is also on show. Some equipment stored in the Depot is owned by the supporting Liverpool Locomotive Preservation Group.

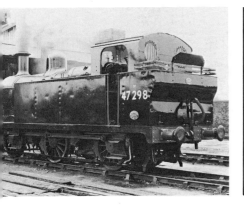

Address Steamport Southport Ltd, Derby Rd, Southport, Lancs, PR9 0TY. Tel. Southport 30693

Enquiries to Above address

Opening times Every weekend afternoon, all year. Also weekdays, June to mid-September. Steamings, Bank Holidays weekends and other special dates

How to get there *By road* A565 to Southport. *By rail* to Southport Chapel St BR

Facilities Car park, refreshments and souvenir shop

Discounts for families

TOP Avonside 0–6–0 saddle tank No. 1568 *Lucy* on brake van rides at Steamport Southport.

CENTRE Ex-LMS 4–6–0 No. 44806 *Magpie*.

BOTTOM LEFT No. 47298 ex-LMS 0–6–0 tank outside Steamport Shed.

Keighley and Worth Valley Railway

The preserved steam railway in the North of England which has everything going for it must be the 5 mile branch line from Keighley station on British Rail's main line from Leeds to Carlisle. It climbs steeply southwards into the Brontë Country, a key tourist area, as a complete working branch route fully equipped with all the things railway enthusiasts and tourists with a touch of nostalgia find agreeable.

Reopened in 1968 by a well organized preservation society, it has had over a decade of experience in building up a system which attracts up to 150,000 passengers a year. In fact it handles so much traffic that British Rail benefits considerably on its Leeds to Keighley service, and as a result the National system co-operates with connections and facilities at Keighley.

There are more than 30 steam locomotives on the line, some of them very famous. The first British 'Atlantic' type 4–4–2 engine, *Sir Henry Oakley*, from the National Railway Museum, and a former Southern Railway 'West Country Pacific', the 4–6–2 *City of Wells* both work on the line. Recently imported from Poland is a big freight engine which was one of the 2–8–0 American-built post-war rehabilitation locomotives, while another American-built engine is a former 0–6–0 dock tank which saw service at Southampton during the D-Day operations. The line also

An American-built 2–8–0 locomotive on the Keighley and Worth Valley Railway.

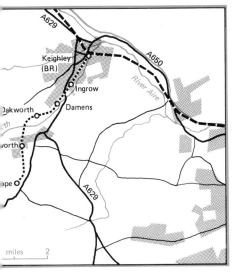

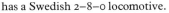

has a Swedish 2–8–0 locomotive.

All trains work up steep hills, go through two tunnels, cross a viaduct, pass from industrial scenery to very rural settings, and call at delightful little country stations. Millions of people loved watching the Keighley and Worth Valley at work (even if they did not know the details) when they saw the film *The Railway Children*, which was made on the route. Several other films and TV plays have used the branch, including a recent Sherlock Holmes movie, for which an early Lancashire and Yorkshire Barton Wright goods engine was restored and given to the railway. The latest film made on the line was *Yanks,* using the big Polish 2–8–0.

The line never closes completely, even operating steam-hauled 'Santa Specials' on certain days in December.

Trains leave from Platform 3 at Keighley, passing Ingrow Halt at 1¼ miles out, Damens at 2 miles, Oakworth station (base for the *Railway Children*) at 2¾ miles, Haworth (where the main shed and works are situated) at 3½ miles and terminate at Oxenhope, 4¾ miles. The ride takes 21 minutes, or a little longer if the optional stops at the halts are made. Limited winter Sunday services shuttle between Oxenhope and Haworth, 10 minutes for the 1¼ miles. Comfortable authentic passenger rolling stock is used.

Oakworth Station received a top award for 1979 in a national contest to find the best kept station among Britain's preserved railways.

There is a prestige 'Pullman Super Train' available for parties, with full catering and bar service. At Oxenhope there is a Locomotive Display and a relics section.

The Keighley and Worth Valley sends out news sheets every month about its activities and has a considerable following overseas, including America, where it has a mutual relationship with AMTRAK, the quasi-nationalized Passenger Rail Corporation.

There are a few works diesels on the line and occasionally two German-built railbuses may operate traffic, but in the main, this is a perfect example of a standard gauge North of England steam branch line which was in public service until closure under the Beeching Butchery in 1962.

Ex-LMS 4–6–0 No. 45212 on the Keighley and Worth Valley Railway.

Address Keighley and Worth Valley Railway Ltd, Haworth Station, Haworth, Keighley, West Yorks, BD22 8NJ. Tel. Haworth 43629

Enquiries to Above address. Timetable available

Opening times All year, weekends and Bank Holidays. Daily, July and August

How to get there *By road* A650 from Leeds and Bradford, M62 via A629. West Yorkshire metro bus. *By rail* to Keighley BR, frequent daily service

Facilities Car park, refreshments and souvenir shop (at Haworth)

Discounts Children and OAPs half-price

Middleton Railway Trust

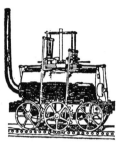

The Middleton Railway in Leeds is standard gauge and traces its direct descent from 1758 when an Act of Parliament created what was the first legislated railway in the world. A horse-drawn freight line then, running for two miles, it has changed but little in the course of two centuries apart from the addition of mechanical haulage. In this matter it can claim the first successful use of steam traction, dating from 1812, 13 years before the Stockton and Darlington ran. Today the Middleton is a registered charity as well as being a limited company, and associated with it is the Steam Power Trust 1965.

The line has a freight run actually earning commercial revenue, hauling goods as and when offered by friendly local factories to the Balm Road sidings of British Railways. The route is some two miles long, but the normal passenger run for visitors is about half this, operated at weekends and on Bank Holidays. The round trip takes about 20 minutes.

The experience is totally different from the usual rural steam journey. Here the atmosphere is industrial, and there is the

BELOW LEFT 0–4–0 saddle tank *Henry de Lacy II* hauling a charter special.

RIGHT Four-wheeled VB Sentinel, No. 54, built in 1933.

nostalgic sound of engines puffing, sending plumes of smoke over grimy factory buildings and across small terraced houses. Tunstall Road Halt is the starting point. The line climbs steeply in places, and the all-volunteer staff must jump down and open gates or switch points from time to time. At Middleton Park Gates the passenger run ends and the engine either backs the train down to Tunstall Road or runs around the train to haul it back. Accommodation is in brake vans or covered waggons, an LNER ballast brake having some seats, but standing is the usual way of travelling.

The engine hauling the short train of waggons and brake van, when I rode the Middleton Railway for the first time, was a Sentinel. It hardly looked like a steam engine, being encased and box-like, a 0–4–0 in fact, but it made the right noises and produced that unmistakable smell. The Trust has a number of small industrial steam engines, most of them 0–4–0s and dating from the 1930s but with at least three of 1940s construction. The waggons are older than the tractive power and a

small Great Western Railway steam crane dates from 1880.

Leeds University Union Railway and Transport Society owns one of the diesel engines, a Hunslett of 1935. It also has two steam engines in the Steam Power Trust based on the Middleton Railway. A curious engine belonging to this Trust is a German Railways 0–4–0 well tank dating from 1895.

There is action on the Middleton from Easter to the end of September (all year round on a freight basis which may be watched), and for visitors well into middle age it is perhaps the only opportunity to recall what industrial steam scenes were like in the time of their youth.

Address Middleton Railway Trust Ltd, Garnet Rd, Leeds, LS11 5JY

Enquiries to Above address

Opening times Easter to end September, weekends and Bank Holidays only, 14.00–16.30 (trains run at half-hourly intervals

How to get there *By road* M1, exit 45, right at Tunstall Rd, or A653. *By rail* to Leeds BR. Buses Nos 74 or 76 from Park Row (City Square) to Tunstall Rd roundabout

Facilities Car park, refreshments and souvenir shop

Discounts Children half-price

TOP LEFT 0–4–0 well tank built in 1893 for Danish State Railways.

RIGHT 0–4–0 tank No. 1310, built in 1891, on brake van service.

BOTTOM Peckett 0–4–0 saddle tank, built in 1941, at Middleton Park Gates.

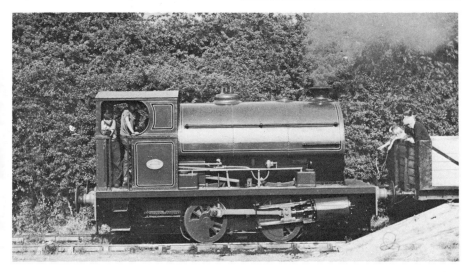

Ravenglass and Eskdale Railway

The 15 inch gauge *Ratty* is to the North of England what the Romney, Hythe and Dymchurch is to the South – a miniaturized working passenger-carrying railway serving a scenic and sparsely populated area as a tourist attraction and transport medium. It links the Cumbrian Coast with the head of a mountainous valley, running for 7 miles from Ravenglass station (junction with British Rail's Cumbrian Coast diesel services) to Eskdale (Dalegarth). The ride is spectacular, with mountains soon encroaching on both sides, and takes about 40 minutes uphill, 35 minutes downhill.

Normally, there are frequent services, steam-hauled, from late March to late October, but there is an all-year round weekday train which serves as basic transport for people in the Valley to reach Ravenglass in the morning for work and return in the afternoon. This train is usually one coach headed by a small diesel.

The railway has a long history, having been constructed in 1875 as a 3ft gauge mineral line for iron ore traffic. A year later, passengers were carried, and this business continued long after the closure of the mines at Boot (Cumberland). The 'Ratty' failed in 1913 and lay abandoned for two years, but despite problems in the First

World War, Narrow Gauge Railways Ltd took it over, converted it to 15 in gauge (11 years before the Romney, Hythe and Dymchurch was built), and carried both tourists and quarry stone from a newly opened Beckfoot Quarry.

Despite closure during the Second World War business remained good until the late 1950s when, with Beckfoot Quarry exhausted and insufficient tourist traffic (probably due to inadequate funds for promotion), the railway closed again. It was saved by members of the Ravenglass and Eskdale Preservation Society, and some generous donations, the largest being from the Daily Telegraph, and since 1960 it has worked extremely well, carrying 2½ million passengers in 20 years.

Ravenglass has become quite a tourist centre thanks to the little railway. Passengers coming off the BR diesel units (running between Carlisle, Whitehaven and Barrow) have plenty to interest them before they ride the 'Ratty'. The display units are fascinating, including two restored Pullman cars, two camping coaches let to visitors, a shop and café, and a pub converted from the former mail line station house. This belongs to the Ravenglass and Eskdale and is called, naturally, 'Ratty Arms'.

A new steam engine was delivered to the line as recently as 1976, named *Northern Rock* after the insurance company which aided her construction. She is a 2–6–2 tender locomotive. The biggest engine is the 2–8–2 *River Mite*, built in 1966, and the oldest is *River Irt*, originally a 0–8–0 tank from 1894 but completely reconstructed at Ravenglass in 1927 into a 0–8–2 tender engine. The 2–8–2 *River Esk* was built in 1923. These locomotives handle the bulk of the summer tourist traffic, in fine weather hauling open carriages. There are some diesels, however, including a miniaturized main line one called *Shelagh of Eskdale*, built like a BR diesel hydraulic in 1968. About 20 closed saloon bogie

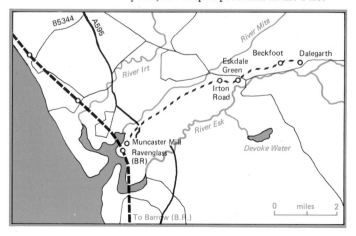

coaches are used in unfavourable weather conditions.

There are plenty of freight wagons for use in maintenance and for uplifting revenue freight along the line, and a Kerr Stuart 0–4–0 well tank (1901) does some shunting. There is also a small 0–4–4 diesel tractor.

After what is one of the finest small train rides in the world, exhilarating on a fine day in an open carriage, the terminus at Eskdale (Dalegarth) affords excellent walking, a good picnic area, car parks, cafés and shops. One way riders can go on by car into the Lake District.

The Preservation Society has volunteers at work and is closely involved, owning the 2–8–2 *River Mite*, and trains are operated by the Ravenglass and Eskdale Railway Company, which owns much of the traction and rolling stock. It is a blend which works and gives a great deal of pleasure to at least 130,000 passengers a year.

Address Ravenglass and Eskdale Railway Co Ltd, Ravenglass, Cumberland, CA18 1SW. Tel. Ravenglass 266

Enquiries to Above address. Timetable available

Opening times End March to end October, 07.45–19.20 (high season)

How to get there *By road* Off A595 Barrow to Whitehaven. One mile east of Ravenglass. *By rail* to Ravenglass BR

Facilities Shop, café and pub at Ravenglass. Car parks, cafés, picnic area and shops at Dalegarth

Special attractions The Railway Museum and Muncaster Water Mill

Discounts For families and groups. Children half-price

TOP *River Esk* and *Northern Rock* meet under the footbridge at Ravenglass.

CENTRE *River Irt* passes Muncaster Mill with a special excursion train.

LEFT *Northern Rock* passes Miteside Halt.

National Railway Museum, York

When the National Collection of railway engines, rolling stock and relics was moved from various places, including Clapham in London, to the former steam depot just on the north side of York station, there were some protests. But the magnificent job which has been made of the Museum soon stilled the protesters. A vast work of reconstruction and assembly was undertaken, with the result that this is not only the finest collection of railwayana in the world but one of its greatest museums.

There was a Railway Museum at York before this, but it was on the south side of the station and not rail connected. The new one, many times the size of the former, and built around a large turntable, is rail linked. Engines can and do come out of it, to run on special trains or travel to other centres on loan. Rail-lovers can now say of the engines at York that they are 'sleeping and not dead'.

The beauty of York is that considerable changes in the exhibits are made from month to month. There is an enormous Reserve Collection, being added to all the time, housed in a former carriage shed, also rail linked. Under the much respected Curator, Dr Coiley, York Museum always has something new to offer the visitor. The Museum has received the highest commendation award from the British Tourist Authority. It attracts visitors from all over the world.

Some exhibits are static and always on display, such as Great Northern single driver No. 1, and some other very early locomotives, as well as relics on the walls. Lectures and films are shown and some displays are geared to events, such as the Centenary of Electric Traction in 1979. Royal saloons from various Sovereigns are among the rolling stock usually accessible. Engines are often on loan from Preservation Societies, and vice-versa.

The collection of early North Eastern Railway engines is a constant delight and rarely changed. The former LBSCR

0–4–2 *Gladstone*, saved from scrap in 1929 and the first privately preserved engine offered to York, is more or less a permanent exhibit.

A great favourite carriage of mine, not always on show, is the Midland third class dining-car with its oak bogies and plush atmosphere, a true reminder of how good the quality was in pre-war days for even the humblest traveller who could afford 'half a crown' for a three course meal.

There is a major annual event at York Museum every October lasting two days, with an auction of surplus railwayana.

Derwent Valley Railway

Address National Railway Museum, Leeman Rd, York. Tel. York 21261

Enquiries to Above address

Opening times Daily 10.00–18.00, except Sundays 14.30–18.00, every day except Christmas and New Year. Admission free

How to get there *By road* to the north side of York BR station. *By rail* to York BR, short walk from BR station

Facilities Car park (off Leeman Rd), cafeteria, shops with books, postcards, sounds of steam records and so on for sale

The Derwent Valley is a quite unique railway, a short line operating out of York which somehow escaped the Grouping of 1923 and even escaped Nationalisation in 1948. It is normally freight only (the last regular passenger services ceased in 1926) and it makes money, actually paying a dividend to its small number of fortunate shareholders. The Derwent Valley owns two small Drewry diesels and several wagons for its freight work. Although under the Light Railway Order and therefore limited to 25 miles an hour, the DVR is standard gauge. For a few summer seasons it carried passengers once daily behind a borrowed tank engine called *Joem*. These services have now ended.

Address Derwent Valley Railway, Layerthorpe Station, York. Tel. York 58981

Enquiries to Above address

How to get there *By road* ½ mile from centre of York, Hill Field Rd off Layerthorpe. *By rail* to York BR

LEFT Part of the National Railway Museum's magnificent collection.

BELOW *Joem* heads a Derwent Valley train.

Yorkshire Dales Railway

ABOVE Signal at Embsay Station, on the Yorkshire Dales Railway.

FAR RIGHT No. 22, Barclay locomotive, hauling NER 1896 Director's Saloon.

It has taken ten years hard work (a booklet is available on the railway called 'Ten Years Hard') to attain the limited preservation situation at Embsay Station, in Yorkshire's Airedale. Perhaps the Yorkshire Dales Railway Co Ltd was optimistic in hoping to be the Dales opposite number of the highly successful 18 mile long Moors line. Geography and competition have been against it.

But at Embsay station, near Skipton, volunteers have created an interesting layout, and operate trains on Sundays in summer over about a mile of track. It is hoped that this will be extended eventually to Bolton Abbey, a famed beauty spot and historic site about 8 miles away. Much money and more labour (a good deal of it skilled) will be needed, together with some co-operation from British Rail and the local Councils.

Embsay was a Midland Railway branch station, out of Skipton on the Grassington line. It is attractive, with an overbridge,

Address Yorkshire Dales Railway Museum Trust, Embsay Station, Embsay, Nr Skipton, N. Yorks. Tel. Skipton 4727

Enquiries to J. R. Ellis, Publicity Officer, at above address. Timetable available

Opening times All year at weekends. Trains operate Easter to December, every Sunday high season, less often at other times

How to get there *By road* A59 Skipton to Harrogate, 1 mile from Skipton. *By rail* to Skipton BR

Facilities Car park, waiting room/café, souvenir and book shop

Special attractions Small Relics Museum, 9½ in gauge steam ride some Sundays

Discounts For groups, on application. Children half-price

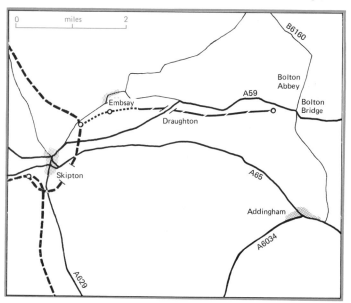

good stone buildings, and some rolling
stock in sidings. Currently, the Dales
Railway is going in for small industrial
steam engines, in both static and active
form, and hopes to lay several gauges to
allow displays of various types. It does,
however, possess a big ex-L M S R 2–8–0
8F freight engine among its collection of
Hunslet and Hudswell Clarke saddle
tanks. There are fourteen steam engines,
three or four small diesels, three good bogie
passenger coaches, a Pullman car and –
used on trip trains and pride of the system –
a North Eastern Railway inspection
saloon from 1896.

King Tut, a 9½ in gauge 2–4–2 tender
engine, built in 1932, is a popular attraction
on summer Sundays, running on a short
stretch of track as a large model display.
There is ample car parking around Embsay
station, and a good waiting room-cum-café
where they make refreshingly strong tea.

Bolton Abbey is a major tourist
attraction in the Airedale region and
visitors will find it rewarding to come out
from there to Embsay until such time as
the Dales Railway can carry them to the
Abbey itself.

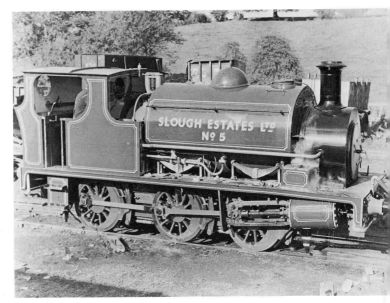

ABOVE Recently restored
Hudswell Clarke 0–6–0
saddle tank *Slough Estates
Ltd No. 5* at Embsay
Station.

LEFT 'Rights of Way' sign.

BELOW *Slough Estates* with
a train on the Yorkshire
Dales Railway.

Steamtown Carnforth

The greatest concentration of active steam locomotives in the North of England, the Carnforth Engine Shed, still in use by British Railways until the very end of scheduled steam in August 1968, is a Mecca for rail fans. It is also a fascinating place to visit for those who have a warm spot in their hearts for the giants of yesterday's tracks, although they know little about them, and for young children who may never have seen the real thing close up.

Carnforth Shed is comparatively modern, possessing still the various facilities needed for overhauling and repairing large steam engines. Approached off the Wharton Road in this North-West Lancashire town, it is called Steamtown Railway Museum, and is well signposted. Inside and out live some 27 steam locomotives, many of them world famous, and a few of them foreign.

Steamtown is open daily, with steam-ups between Easter and October. The Carnforth Shed provides engines for British Rail's own regular summer steam specials around the Cumbrian Coast via Ulverston and Barrow-in-Furness, and may be very active on the appropriate days. On some weekdays in summer there may be no steam action, although a vintage steam crane could be moving about at work.

At any time however, the Museum area is full of interest and the great engines may be examined. They will include the legendary 4472 *Flying Scotsman*, the former Southern Railway's *Lord Nelson*, and the same Company's Pacific *Canadian Pacific*, a big French Pacific 231 (K22), and German Railways 01 class Pacific No. 1104, an ex-LNER 'Green Arrow' and a Thompson B1. There are several ex-

Ex-LNER 2–6–2 No. 4771 *Green Arrow*.

LMS 'Black Fives' and the Great Western is represented by Hall class 4–6–0 *Raveningham Hall*. A number of smaller engines are there, too, plus some fine examples of rolling stock, including a buffet car and two Pullmans, *Rosalind* and *Padua*, built in 1921, with six-wheeled bogies.

There are good refreshment facilities in part of the huge shed, and the gift and souvenir shop is the best equipped I have encountered on any preserved steam railway or base in Britain.

Address Steamtown Railway and Museum, Warton Rd, Carnforth, Lancs. Tel. Carnforth 4220

Enquiries to Above address. Timetable available

Opening times Museum open daily all year (except Christmas). Trains operate Sundays, Easter to October, daily July and August for passenger service, 11.00–17.00

How to get there *By road* A6/M6 exit 35, then follow signs. *By rail* to Carnforth BR

Facilities Car park, refreshments, picnic area and excellent souvenir shop

Special attractions OO model railway and Midland signal box

Discounts For families and groups. Reduced rate for children

ABOVE Ex-LNER 4–6–2 No. 4472 Flying Scotman.

LEFT Ex-LNER Gresley Pacific, No. 4498, *Sir Nigel Gresley*.

Lakeside and Haverthwaite Railway

Lake Windermere, largest lake in England and Wales, has been a great tourist attraction since Wordsworth's time. One British Railways Sealink vessel used at peak holiday periods, the *Teal,* based at Lakeside, dates back closer to the famous Lake District poet's era than the present day. It seemed a tragedy when the British Rail link to its own veteran steamer was severed after a century of operation at the end of 1965.

Enthusiasts soon got together, however, and as the Lakeside Railway Society founded in 1967 proposed reopening the branch from Plumpton Junction on the Barrow-in-Furness line. Sadly, due to lack of funds and other problems, the whole length could not be re-established, and the Society had to be content with saving the 3¼ miles of line between Haverthwaite Station and Lakeside, via Newby Bridge, an intermediate wayside station. This was achieved by 1973, services beginning over Easter in that year.

The Lakeside and Haverthwaite Railway Co Ltd (supported by the Lakeside Railway Society) now takes large numbers of tourists over its short stretch of line to the cruise vessels on Windermere, with combined rail and boat tickets available. The trains are usually steam-hauled from a selection of twelve locomotives, but the Company also owns two diesels, mainly for maintenance work.

Formerly a branch of the Furness Railway, noted for its blue engines, the Lakeside line is single track standard gauge, passing through leafy, hilly country to the southern shore of Windermere. The ride takes about 15 minutes, and recaptures the atmosphere of the late 1940s and 1950s rather than earlier periods of railway history. The best motive power consists of two Fairburn 2–6–4 tank engines built in 1950 and 1951 respectively, to former LMS designs. These haul British Railways Mark 1 coaches from the early 1950s and look absolutely authentic as branch trains

from the era just before closure. There are, however, 0–6–0 industrial tank engines dating from 1919 and 1929. One of the small diesels, a 0–4–0 called *Fluff,* predates the latest steam engine (a Hunslet 0–6–0 saddle tank) by 16 years.

Haverthwaite station is headquarters of the railway, with a small closed locomotive shed and some equipment stored in the open.

This is an extremely pleasant little railway, not as well known as it should be, catering mostly to people heading for a day out on Lake Windermere who know about the short steam train trip, or hear about it while on holiday in the Lake District. Both the run and the support would be immensely improved if by some near miracle the old track could be restored to allow trains all the way to Plumpton Junction and on to Ulverston station, well served by British Rail trains and open to regular steam specials whose motive power is supplied from Steamtown Carnforth (see page 124).

Address Lakeside and Haverthwaite Railway, Haverthwaite Station, Ulverston, Cumbria, LA12 8AL. Tel. Newby Bridge 594

Enquiries to As above. Timetable available

Opening times Easter, Sundays until May, daily May to end September, weekends in October. See timetable for details

How to get there *By road* A590 to Haverthwaite. *By rail* to Grange or Ulverston BR

Facilities Car park, refreshments and gift shop at Haverthwaite

Special attractions Connection with Sealink steamers at Lakeside for Bowness and Ambleside, combined tickets available

Discounts For groups of 10 or more. Reduced rate for children

Bowes Railway

In the same hilly area of South Tyneside in County Durham as the Tanfield Railway (see page 134), the Bowes Railway has the advantage of support by the Tyne and Wear Industrial Monuments Trust. It is a mixture of old waggonways, steam-hauled colliery lines and rope haulage.

John Bowes built the railway, but it did not carry his name until 1932, 92 years after he had laid the tracks from the re-opened coal pit at Marley Hill. Springwell, near Gateshead, is where the railway relics and short steam runs may be enjoyed. There is a standard gauge engine shed with three steam engines and two coaches, also a museum.

The Rocket replica (for steaming at the 150 years Rainhill spectacular in 1980) was constructed at Springwell Works.

Over at Blackham's hill there are occasional demonstrations of the rope haulage of coal tips, and one may see historic workshops.

Barclay saddle tank No. 2274 and Rope Reel Waggon.

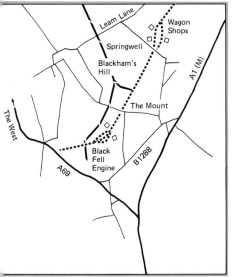

Address Bowes Railway, Springwell Village, Gateshead, 9. Tel. Washington 461847

Enquiries to Tyne and Wear Industrial Monuments Trust, Sandyford House, Archbold Terrace, Newcastle-upon-Tyne, NE2 1ED. Tel. Washington 816144

Opening times Bank Holiday Sundays and Mondays (Easter Monday to August) and first Sundays, July to October. Operating days, 12.00–17.30, Static (most weekends), 10.30–16.30

How to get there *By road* B1288 Wrekenton to Washington, Springwell Village, 4 miles south-east of Gateshead. *By rail* to Newcastle Central/Sunderland BR

Facilities Car park, café and shop (on operating days only)

Special attractions Unique rope haulage demonstrations and tours of railway's own historic workshops.

Discounts Children half-price

Darlington North Road Station Museum

The oldest station in the world at which trains still stop for passengers is the North Road at Darlington, on the present Darlington (Bank Top) to Bishop Auckland line. More than 150 years ago, it was part of the Stockton and Darlington Railway, first public passenger-carrying railway in the world, whose line ran through North Road on the way between Shildon, County Durham, and the Tees at Stockton.

Two tracks run to platforms at the back of North Road, but the major part of the station has been restored, complete with Doric pillars outside, and filled with what can only be described as treasures. The engine that hauled the first passenger train has a place of honour inside. This is, of course, Stockton and Darlington 0–4–0 No. 1, *Locomotion,* which had an active life on the nearby tracks from 1825 to 1846, and in later years spent half a century on a plinth at Darlington Bank Top station.

The younger S & D R engine, 0–6–0 *Derwent,* which stood for so long beside *Locomotion* on the Bank Top plinth, is alongside again, in the hallowed hall of North Road.

Completing the flavour of the North Eastern Railway and its antecedents are two other engines, a 0–6–0 from 1875 and a Fletcher 2–4–0 express engine from 1885. There are goods and passenger waggons also arranged on two tracks inside the hall, while around the walls are relics, maps, posters, timetables and other material associated with the North Eastern Railway. Other railway systems also get a small showing.

Grant aided by the English Tourist Board and commended officially by the British Tourist Authority, North Road receives more visitors from foreign countries than from Britain. It seems the local people do not support it very well, either from ignorance or neglect. However, it is a splendid tribute to early railways and should be seen by anyone going to the North-East of England where railways were born.

In former waiting rooms and offices there is a good souvenir shop and the curator's bureau. Admission is nominal, while souvenir platform tickets are sold from machines for small coins.

Ex-NER 0–6–0 No. 1275 in front; behind Ex-NER 2–4–0 No. 1463, built in 1885 and S&DR 0–4–0 No. 1 *Locomotion,* built 1825.

Address Darlington North Road Station Museum, Station Rd, Darlington, Co. Durham. Tel. Darlington 60532
Enquiries to Above address
Opening times Monday to Saturday, 10.00, Sunday afternoons in summer
How to get there *By road* on A167 to Durham ½ mile from town centre. *By rail* Direct to Darlington North Road BR
Facilities Free car park outside main entrance, souvenir shop. No refreshments, but several cafés within ½ mile

West Lancashire Light Railway

Monkwearmouth Station Museum

Located near Hesketh Bank is a short length of 2 ft gauge railway built by narrow gauge enthusiasts, largely for their own amusement, but visitors are welcome at their own risk. It starts its run from Becclesall, close to Station Road, Hesketh Bank, and runs just over $\frac{1}{4}$ mile but it is expected to be extended.

The first 300 yards were laid in 1967 and the little railway gives a home to a collection of small industrial diesels and two steam engines, one of them a 0–4–0 saddle tank built by Hunslet in 1903, which saw considerable service on the famous and now defunct Dinorwic slate quarries near Llanberis. The other steam engine, which is likely to be in service on summer weekends, is a 0–6–0 Kerr Stuart tank dating from 1915. Two 20-seater passenger coaches are from the Southport Pier Railway.

Admission is free to the static exhibits (they include a number of aged Simplex industrial diesels) but the railway does not set out to cater especially for the public.

Address West Lancashire Light Railway, Station Rd, Hesketh Bank, Nr Preston, Lancs.

Enquiries to The Hon Secretary, West Lancashire Light Railway, 790 Ormskirk Rd, Pemberton, Wigan, Lancs, WN5 8AX. Tel. Wigan 218078

Opening times All year, Sunday afternoons, 13.30–17.30

How to get there *By road* A59, unclassified from Tarleton. *By rail* to Southport or Preston BR

Facilities Free car park and refreshments

Discounts Reduced rate for children

A charming and elegant station on the Newcastle to Sunderland line, Monkwearmouth was designed by the noted Sunderland architect Thomas Moore on the orders of George Hudson, the 'Railway King'. Closed to local traffic, the station sees diesel trains passing through on their way between the Tyne and Wear cities.

The station itself has been turned into a museum administered by the Tyne and Wear Museums Service and is completely restored, its imposing classical facade cleaned and its elegant rooms refurbished. Displays and photographs and posters may be viewed inside, while outside at a disused platform are typical porters' trolleys, trunks and cases, and tin advertisements. Two items of rolling stock are on the line: a North Eastern Railway brake van and a River Wear Commissioners side-tip wagon. In the goods yard opposite, not yet open to the public, is a tank engine and some waggons, awaiting restoration.

Inside the station there are wax figures of a booking clerk, the station master, and a male passenger of the late Victorian period. There was a lady passenger but a curious visitor to the Museum used to come in every day and hold her wax hand for ten minutes. This eventually fell off and the figure toppled! It has not been reinstated. Just south of the section where the lines cross the Wear is T. E. Harrison's wrought-iron hog-back girder bridge dating from 1879, the largest surviving single span bridge of its kind in the world.

Address Monkwearmouth Station Museum, North Bridge St, Sunderland. Tel. Sunderland 77075

Enquiries to Above address

Opening times Daily, all year. Admission free

How to get there *By road* A19 Sunderland to South Shields. *By rail* to Sunderland BR

Facilities Car park

Isle of Man Railways

Much larger than the Isle of Wight, Man is big enough to have a vintage transport system, running more or less continuously for 30 miles along its eastern shore. It is virtually a living transport museum, with steam trains, horse trams, and ancient electric train-trams operating in association with each other.

Isle of Man officials did not recognize the public and tourist interest in their elderly and attractive methods of transport until the end of the 1950s. The Isle of Man Railway was run as a normal system, as was the Manx Electric Railway, with big paid staffs and management. They lost money, and all but disappeared before more enlightened views pressed by the Isle of Man Tourist Board prevailed. Some enchanting railway lines, such as Douglas to Peel and St. John's to Ramsey, were lost in the early 1960s due to inaction at the time. In 1968, £20,000 was needed to save Isle of Man Railways, but the Marquis of Ailsa, who took on the entire railway, had to withdraw after losing more than £25,000 of his own money.

Volunteers and enthusiasts were almost actively discouraged in the 1950s and early 1960s. The railway ran as part of the Isle of Man Bus Company and though the General Manager, Mr W. Lambden actively promoted the railway for its tourist activities, he was compelled to pay more attention to his buses.

Today, the steam railway, after several changes of administration, seems secure, running on its 3 ft gauge from Douglas to Port Erin, a distance of fractionally over 15 miles. Yet for reasons by no means properly explained, there are no trains on Saturdays. Although Saturdays are busy 'bed-changing' days, when holidaymakers from England, Wales and Ireland are coming or going, there must be visitors spending two weeks in the island or taking their holidays from Sunday to Sunday who would enjoy a train excursion.

There is now an Isle of Man Railway Society, largely based outside the island, which helps with funds and supports a museum at Port Erin. The Society has put up money for repainting a locomotive and owns one or two items of vintage rolling stock. Memorabilia of a former constituent company, the Manx Northern, are displayed.

No. 8 *Fenella*, built in 1894, at Castletown on the 3 ft gauge.

Douglas terminus station is a big, handsome red-brick building, well-sited near the harbour and the business streets. Developers have wanted it for years. Sometimes the trains are put out to Ballasalla, or another departure point along the line, leaving the palm-lined platforms empty.

Pulling out of Douglas there is a steep climb to wooded country, and then follows a series of switchback gradients to Ballasalla. It is 1 in 65 up towards Port Soderick and 1 in 60 down to Ballasalla. At Castletown the line is close enough to the sea to give glimpses of it shimmering to the east, and through fairly level water meadows the ride becomes quite fast by any standard. The last half mile from Port St Mary to Port Erin is picturesque as the hilly southern corner of the island is approached. The run lasts about an hour and all stations are stopped at, but on some sections the running can be faster than is customary on narrow gauge in Britain. Almost all passengers are holidaymakers; in recent years the Manx have not supported the railway to the extent of riding on it.

Only five of the delightful little Beyer Peacock 2–4–0 tank engines are still working, out of a stock of eleven. These include the second oldest, *Loch*, No. 4, built in 1874, and the newest, *Kissack*, No. 13, built in 1910. Some 20 carriages are in use, all in good shape and quite comfortable compartment stock. There are no diesels, but two railcars (bought from Northern Ireland about 20 years ago for Peel school traffic) are stored.

Address Isle of Man Railways, Terminus Building, Strathallan Crescent, Douglas, Isle of Man. Tel. 4549

Enquiries to Above address. Timetable available

Opening times Frequent daily (except Saturdays) service, May to September. Some peak season special excursions on Saturdays

How to get there *By sea* to Douglas. *By air* to Ronaldsway Airport and bus to Castleton

Facilities Car park, refreshments and souvenir shop

Discounts Available on request. Children half-price

Special attractions Railway museum at Port Erin

CENTRE No. 13 *Kissack* at Douglas Station.

BOTTOM One of the Isle of Man Railways' Beyer Peacock 2–4–0 tank locomotives hauls a train in the summer season.

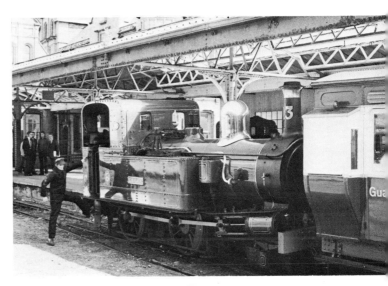

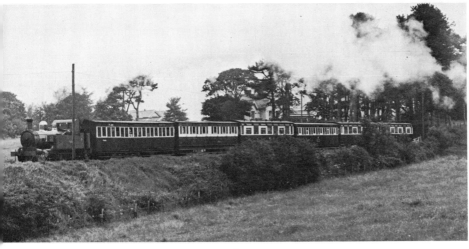

Manx Electric Railway

A vintage Manx Electric tram climbs to Snaefell Summit.

Until a few years ago, you could alight from a steam train at Douglas terminus station, walk a short distance, then join a horse tram for a trip of 1½ miles to Derby Castle, terminus of the Manx Electric. This remains possible but the walk is sometimes increased when steam trains are no longer let in to their proper station.

Horse trams provide a gentle and pleasant interlude along the busy Douglas Promenade. In summer the service is intense with limited trips operated in spring and early autumn, all trams (both open and closed) being hauled by carefully trained Irish horses, one to a tram. Each horse makes two round trips then rests in the Derby Castle stables for four hours. There were 56 horses at last count. Some trams are open toast-racks, others are closed.

Manx Electric vehicles start from beside the stables. They are in most cases older than the horse trams and older than four of the five IOM steam engines. The gauge is 3ft to Ramsey, identical to that used by the IOMR and the horse trams. One power car is said to date from 1893, the year of the opening of the first section from Douglas Derby Castle to Onchan.

There are 24 power cars and 25 trailers at present, some open and some closed. Having made the trip over Laxey Head in a bitter northeasterly blizzard in the late 1950s I appreciated the closed saloon, but there was no heating to speak of. A limited winter service operates today and freight vehicles are often attached, but in the main this is a tourist light railway. One car is credited with carrying King Edward VII, while another is retained and decorated for use by the Bishop of Soder and Man.

Without doubt a ride on the Manx Electric provides the finest maritime cliff scenery in the British Isles, while one section, going off from Laxey, climbs up a mountain! The Snaefell branch grinds uphill beyond the reach of roads to open moorland, coming to a stop barely 70ft below the actual summit of the mountain. On a clear day, passengers may see five countries from the tram-train's windows (England's Lake District, Snowdonia of Wales, the coast of Galloway in Scotland, Northern Ireland's Mountains of Mourne and the hills of Eire). The Manx Electric really has a great deal going for it and it is incredible that it took such a struggle to save it.

Although salvation has come from the

Address Manx Electric Railway, Derby Castle Station, Douglas, Isle of Man. Tel. Douglas 4549

Enquiries to Isle of Man Railways, Terminus Building, Strathallan Crescent, Douglas, Isle of Man. Timetable available

Opening times Frequent daily service, April to September, on Douglas, Laxey, Ramsey line. Snaefell Mountain line, May to end September

How to get there *By sea* to Douglas. *By air* to Ronaldsway Airport and bus

Facilities Car park, refreshments and souvenir shop

Discounts For families and groups. Runabout tickets available

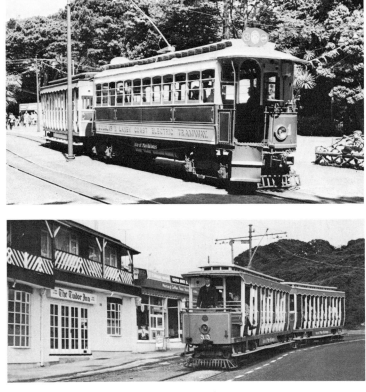

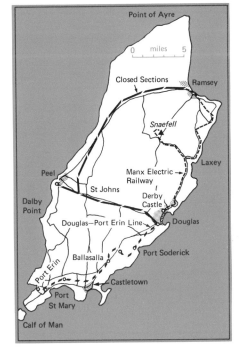

Isle of Man Government and the Tourist Board, a Manx Electrical Railway Society with 200 members (unlike the supporters of the steam railway, most of these are Manxmen) helps with publicity campaigns and maintains close contact with officials about the funding of the system. It also runs a short 3 ft gauge line of its own, the Queen's Pier Tramway at Ramsey, which carries passengers.

Passengers going on the Snaefell Line must change tram-trains at Laxey, for the mountain section is 3 ft 6 in gauge. This line is $4\frac{3}{4}$ miles long and works on a gradient of 1 in 12, the steepest in Britain to use adhesion only, although there is a centre rail on the Fell system for braking on the descent (probably the last example of Fell in the world). The Snaefell line was opened in 1895, and all six of its special cars date from the opening.

It is 18 miles from Derby Castle to Ramsey, a journey taking about 75 minutes. The ride from Laxey to Snaefell is about 35 minutes. The Ramsey route has an all-year service, very sparce in winter between Laxey and Ramsey.

TOP LEFT Cars Nos. 27–25 at Derby Castle sheds.

TOP RIGHT Manx Electric Railway Car No. 1, built in 1894, at Laxey.

CENTRE Car 33 and trailer at Onchan en route for Douglas Derby Castle Terminus.

Tanfield Railway

Amid the high country to the South of the River Tyne is the cradle of civil engineering as we know it today. Coal production gave birth to waggon transport on primitive rails, and in the Tanfield area of County Durham there was built the

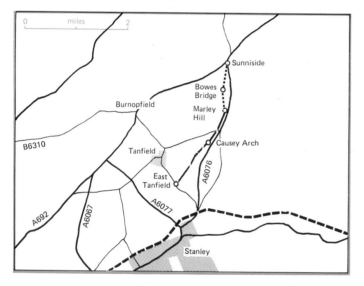

world's first railway bridge, the Causey Arch. It stands today, after decades of neglect, restored to its former state. Near it, under the shadow of Marley Hill Colliery (where the largest fleet of pit ponies at work in the North East may be found), is the headquarters of the Railway.

The Tanfield Way has moved coal for 300 years and the railway itself can be traced back to the Ravensworth Waggonway of 1669. Horses were the traction for nearly 200 years, then stationary steam winding engines, and finally steam locomotives, from 1881 to closure in 1964.

Three miles of the old waggonway between Sunniside and East Tanfield are being relaid to form Tyneside's main preserved railway centre. It runs through the wooded Causey Dene and already

passenger trains are running for over a mile. The Tanfield Railway Association (which publishes its own magazine 'Waggonway' as a quarterly) possesses 14 steam locomotives, all of a type associated with colliery lines in the North-East, including an extremely interesting 0–4–0 Sentinel, and one diesel more than 40 years old.

Carriages of the period are being restored slowly at Tanfield base, one of them a North Eastern clerestory found in Hull as a mere shed framework. Meanwhile enthusiasts have built up some coaching stock reminiscent of the kind in which miners travelled to and from shifts.

Tanfield is quite near to Beamish, the vast museum of Durham life and industrial archaeology (see page 135). There is a good relationship, with Beamish spare engines stored at Tanfield. Short of funds, the Tanfield enthusiasts are struggling, but their keenness is infectious and the railway well worth a visit and a ride along historic tracks in a mining landscape unexpectedly interspersed with lovely wooded scenery. This railway will work in close liaison with the Bowes Railway (see page 127).

Address Tanfield Railway, 33 Stocksfield Avenue, Newcastle-upon-Tyne, NE5 2DX. Tel. Newcastle 742002

Enquiries to Above address. Timetable available

Opening times Railway Loco Shed and HQ area open every Sunday for viewing. Steam, Bank Holidays (except Christmas), Easter Sunday and Monday, 1st May, Spring and Summer, Sundays in July and August

How to get there By road Off A6076 Sunniside to Stanley, 5 miles south-west of Gateshead. Buses 701–704 from Marlborough Crescent, Newcastle. By rail to Newcastle Central BR

Facilities Large car park, refreshments and souvenir shop

Discounts Children half-price

North of England Open Air Museum, Beamish

Arranged in the wide acres of Beamish Hall, former seat of the Shafto Family, is the largest industrial outdoor Museum in Britain. It is in the North part of County Durham near Chester-le-Street on former intensive coal mining land.

There is a steam railway running on about a mile of track from the completely transported Rowley station, brought from its old site in a village in the hills beyond Consett. A cast iron footbridge comes from the Newcastle and Carlisle Railway and an 1896 signal box is from Carr House. The last surviving C class 0–6–0 goods engine of the North Eastern Railway hauls a vintage coach for the five minute ride, sometimes replaced by a North Eastern 0–6–0 tank locomotive.

On half a mile of track, vintage trams from Sunderland, Sheffield and Gateshead give rides to visitors. The tram terminus is close to the building housing a remarkable transport collection, pride of which is the original 1822 Hetton locomotive built by George Stephenson, which worked for 90 years at Hetton Colliery and is thought to be among the three oldest steam engines in the world.

Over at a working colliery open to Beamish visitors is the replica of *Locomotion* (original is in Darlington North Road Station Museum) built by Mr Mike Satow in 1975 for 'Rail 150' celebrations at Shildon. It stands, sometimes in steam, with some original pit waggons.

Working horses on a typical farm, steam traction engines, rows of pit cottages with traditional furniture, and many other items tracing the history of County Durham in the 19th century are at Beamish. The largest exhibit is a monster steam shovel, a 100 ton Ruston Bucyrus dating from 1931.

Address North of England Open Air Museum, Beamish, Stanley. Co. Durham. Tel. Stanley 33580

Enquiries to Above address

Opening times Daily, May to August, 10.00–18.00, Tuesdays to Sundays, April and September

How to get there By road Off A693 Chester-le-Street to Stanley Rd. By rail to Durham BR

Facilities Car park, refreshments and souvenir shop

LEFT Unique 0–4–0 colliery locomotive at Beamish.

RIGHT Rowley Station, moved to Beamish from near Consett, with ex-North Eastern 0–6–0 tank engine.

North Yorkshire Moors Railway

In the existing state of railway preservation in Britain, the North Yorkshire Moors Railway (known regionally as 'Moorsrail') is the ultimate. On its relatively long run (18 miles) from Grosmont to Pickering, it has all the attractions of a scenic rural railway, with steep gradients, curves, splendid scenery, and a good long downhill run, lacking only a substantial tunnel for dedicated enthusiasts.

Moorsrail, with the aid of British Rail at its northern end, goes 'from somewhere to somewhere'. It is a journey which can be undertaken for a purpose as well as a round trip for pure pleasure. People do want to travel from Whitby to Pickering and vice-versa. There are buses at Pickering to make onward journeys, to Malton or York.

The preservation line came into being soon after the Beeching Butchery, which cut three of the four lines serving the coastal harbour and seaside resort of Whitby in North Yorkshire. A victim was the Whitby-Pickering-Malton line, giving access to York. The only survivor was the Esk Valley line, from Whitby to Middlesbrough. At a station called Grosmont, in the centre of a small village, the Pickering line verged sharply away to the south. The tracks were not pulled up and a preserva-

tion scheme, greatly aided by the North Eastern Railway Locomotive Preservation Society, set up shop at Grosmont and was soon operating steam trains up the steep 1 in 49 gradient to Goathland, about 3 miles away.

Officially entitled the North Yorks Moors Historical Railway Trust, the undertaking successfully bid for the remainder of the track to Pickering. It was aided by a grant of £38,000 from the English Tourist Board, but a battle followed with the Forestry Commission, which objected to steam locomotives passing through the heavily planted woodlands on the way down (or up) between Ellerbeck Summit beyond Goathland and Pickering. A compromise was finally worked out, allowing a limited number of through steam trains, plus a service of diesel units called 'National Parks Scenic Diesel Service'. Passengers can sample both, changing from steam to diesel at Goathland if desired.

Timetables clearly mark which trains are diesel-hauled and which are steam, also which runs are made with the scenic units. The overall journey takes approximately one hour (compared to 47 minutes in British Rail days), but this allows for the maximum speed of 25 miles an hour laid

0–6–2 No. 5, built for Lambton Colliery, at Grosmont Summit.

down by the Light Railway Order. Climbing the 1 in 49 to Goathland, most trains are only able to make about half this speed, which they do with immensely satisfying eruptive sounds.

In wild scenery close to the summit of the Moors the strange sight of the giant white 'golf balls' of Fylingdales Early Warning System can be viewed to the east. The line climbs through a gorge used by George Stephenson's rope haulage railway laid in 1836. When it was turned into a steam line in 1865, the route was slightly altered and the gradient eased to its present 1 in 49. Newtondale is traversed on the way down to Pickering, with a stop at Levisham.

Good connections are afforded at Grosmont from the Whitby-Middlesbrough BR diesel units, which have prospered thanks to Moorsrail, but steam right through to Whitby is still largely opposed by the authorities. Grosmont village has boomed due to thousands of visitors.

With seventeen steam engines and six diesels, plus thirty-one passenger coaches, there is a great deal of interest at Grosmont. Access to the engine shed is by a path beside the short tunnel northwards from Grosmont station. Among the engines are two extremely powerful 0–6–2 tanks from Lambton Colliery, both capable of taking fully loaded six-coach trains over the summit. There is a Stanier 'Black Five' named *George Stephenson*, two typical North Eastern Railway goods

Address North Yorkshire Moors Historical Railway Trust, Pickering Station, Pickering, North Yorks, YO18 7AJ. Tel. Pickering 72508 and 73535

Enquiries to Above address. Timetable available

Opening times Daily Easter to mid-November, 09.00–18.00. Thursdays only, 09.00–21.30

How to get there *By road* A170 Thirsk-Scarborough. A64 and A169 York-Malton. *By rail* to Grosmont Junction BR

Facilities Large free car parks, refreshment room and static buffet car for hot meals, souvenir and book shops at Grosmont and Pickering

Special attractions Audio-visual room and listening posts

Discounts For families and groups. Reduced rate for children

ABOVE The popular ex-SR 4–6–0 'S15' *Greene King*.

LEFT A 'National Park Scenic Special'.

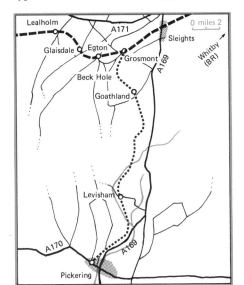

engines, many industrial tanks, a British Rail standard 2–6–4 tank, a Great Northern Railway 0–6–0 saddle tank (privately owned and one of the first engines to be privately purchased), and a 'Western Class' diesel hydraulic retired in 1977 by BR Western Region. Visiting engines also work the line, the most popular one at the time of writing being the former SR 4–6–0 of Class S15 named *Greene King*.

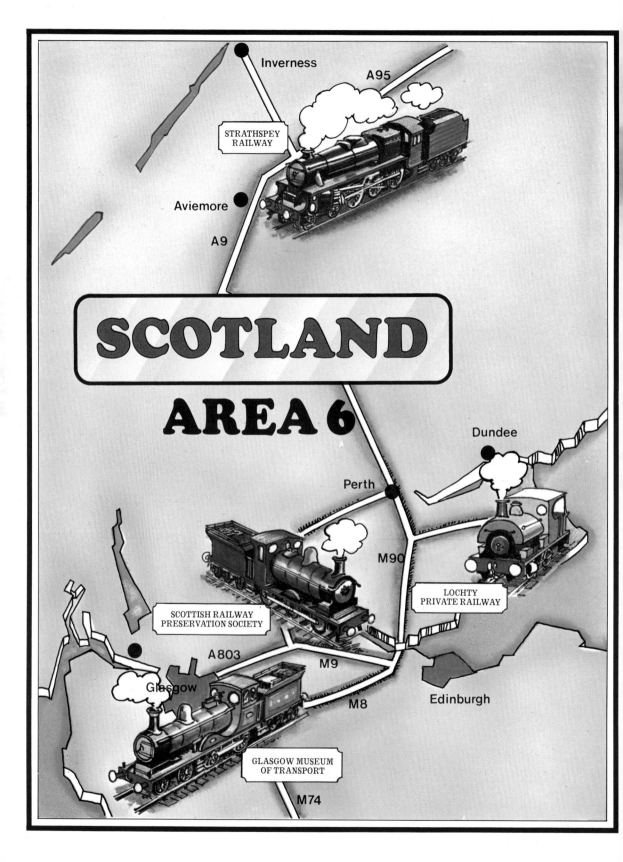

Glasgow Museum of Transport

No-one with any interest in trains or trams, in or near the city of Glasgow, should miss a visit to the Transport Museum out at Albert Drive (the old Coplawhill Works) on the South Side. The exhibits are all static, but the museum has a rich collection of both engines and tramcars. Excellent booklets and historic photographs, even paintings, may be purchased at the well-stocked shop.

Key exhibits are Caledonian No. 123, the beautifully preserved last of the 'single drivers' which worked special trains until 1965, and the Jones Goods of the Highland Railway, Britain's first 4–6–0, built in 1896. The North British Railway is represented by its magnificent 4–4–0 *Glen Douglas,* dating from 1913. The Great North of Scotland Railway is recalled by *Gordon Highlander,* a 4–4–0 used until 1965, built in 1920. Rare indeed is a Glasgow and South Western Railway engine, but the Museum has one, a 0–6–0 tank built in 1917. There is also a standard Caledonian Railway MacIntosh goods engine, one of a class numbering 812, built in 1899.

One or two exhibits may be removed and put into service with preservation groups on a temporary basis, or exchanged. Many models are to be seen and the walls have famous name and number plates.

Address Glasgow Museum of Transport, 25 Albert Drive, Glasgow, GL1 2PE. Tel. Glasgow 423 8000

Enquiries to Above address

Opening times Daily, 10.00–17.00, Sundays, 14.00–17.00. Closed Christmas, 1st January. Admission free

How to get there *By road* to Albert Drive, on South Side. *By rail* to BR Pollokshields East. Underground to Bridge St

Facilities Car parking nearby, refreshment room for light meals and Scottish teas, souvenir shop

ABOVE GNSR 4–4–0 No. 49 *Gordon Highlander.*
LEFT G&SWR 0–6–0 tank No. 9.

BOTTOM HR 4–6–0 No. 103, built in 1896.

Lochty Private Railway

The key attraction of this short standard gauge railway near Anstruther in Fife is the presence of streamlined A4 Gresley Pacific No. 60009, *Union of South Africa,* one of the high speed steam express engines built in 1937 for hauling LNER's *Coronation.*

Not that *Union of South Africa* can show her paces on the Lochty for the line is only 1½ miles long. But it keeps her active and from time to time she is allowed out on Scottish main line tracks with enthusiast's specials. Many thousands of people come to the Lochty to ride behind her on Sunday afternoons in summer.

Mr John B. Cameron is the owner and owner, too, of the farmland through which this section of the former East Fife Railway runs. The railway once went around the Neuk of Fife from Leuchars Junction and St Andrews to Leven and Methil, and there are still track connections for coal traffic enabling the big Pacific to gain access to British Rail metals. The Lochty starts at a point some 6 miles from Crail, on the B940 road from Cupar to Crail. It runs from Lochty to Knightsward station, 1½ miles, but the one-time 100 miles an hour streamliner has to take about 8

minutes for the journey hauling just 2 coaches. However, people come from all over the world to see and enjoy the famous locomotive in steam.

If the big engine should be away preparing for a British Rail trip, there is now other steam motive power at Lochty in the form of a 0–6–0 Bagnall saddle tank (built in 1944) and a veteran 0–4–0 Peckett saddle tank dating from 1915. A small modern diesel completes the motive power, and two coaches are the total of rolling stock.

Address Lochty Private Railway, Lochty Station, Lochty, Fife

Enquiries to The Honorary Secretary, Fife Railway Preservation Group, 48 Hendry Rd, Kirkcaldy, Fife, KY2 5JN. Tel. Kirkcaldy 4587

Opening times Mid-June to early September, Sundays, 14.00–17.00

How to get there *By road* off B940 Cupar to Crail. *By rail* to Cupar (10 miles away)

Facilities Car park and souvenir shop

Discounts For groups of 10 or more. Children half-price

RIGHT AND FAR RIGHT Streamlined A4 Gresley Pacific No. 60009, *Union of South Africa,* based on Lochty Private Railway, works main line specials.

TOP Bagnall 0–6–0 saddle tank No. 16, built in 1944.

CENTRE Peckett 0–4–0 saddle tank, built in 1915.

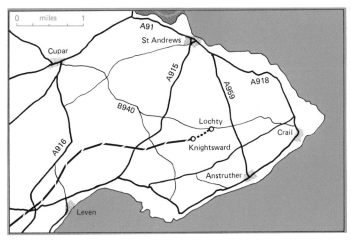

Strathspey Railway

Scotland, despite all its tourism, has very little in the way of preserved steam railways. It is only in the last few years that one of any significant length has opened for business, although the project has been planned for a decade. This is the Strathspey line, running from the popular Highland tourist centre of Aviemore to Boat of Garten, a $5\frac{1}{4}$-mile journey. A thorough job has been done on restoration and it may well prove to be one of the best and longest lasting in Britain. It has every chance of being extended in the years ahead, to reach Grantown-on-Spey, giving it a journey length of $12\frac{3}{4}$ miles and a run through some of the most spectacular scenery in the British Isles.

This was the secondary main line of the old Highland Railway between Aviemore and Forres (for Inverness), closed under the Beeching Butchery of the early 1960s. Money for restoration has been raised

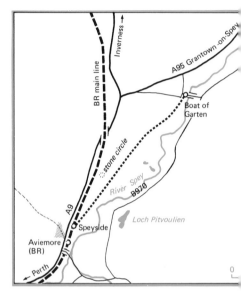

Hunslet 'Austerity' 0–6–0 saddle tank No. 48.

largely by shareholders of the Strathspey Railway Company, but the Highlands and Islands Development Board made a grant of £10,000 in view of the line's contribution to tourism in the Spey Valley.

Steam trains start from Speyside Station, not from the British Rail Station in Aviemore about ¼ mile away. Headquarters are at Boat of Garten Station, where most equipment is based. Timetables are issued, showing the journey taking about 20 minutes on the standard gauge, well-laid track. Pulling away from Speyside station, trains run close to the Highland main line before climbing away at 1 in 175 to the east, with the magnificent summits of the Cairngorms outlined to the right of the train. Forest, mountain, and rushing river are the scenic delights of this 5¼-mile ride through the heart of the Grampian district. The Spey, a mile away at times, is rejoined as the train descends gradually to Boat of Garten in its majestic setting below the Abernethy Forest.

There are ten steam engines and four diesels on the roster, with eighteen passenger coaches. A train gives the very pleasing appearance of a secondary main line express of the early 1950s rather than the deeply nostalgic picture of vintage steam of a bygone age. Three tender engines look purposeful, two of them being Ivatt class 2MT 2–6–0s dating from 1950 and 1952, while the third is a 'Black Five' 4–6–0 Stanier from 1934. Five six-coupled tank engines are relatively modern, three from the National Coal Board. In addition there is a collection of small 0–4–0 tanks (mainly from distilleries) kept at Aviemore. The diesel-mechanical fleet is for work on construction and maintenance; all are small.

There are some goods vehicles and an interesting former Caledonian Railway handcrane dating from 1905. A few sleeping cars of LMS and LNER construction are used as overnight accommodation for volunteers working on the line.

More than 20,000 passengers are hauled during the summer, a figure which should increase as this most northerly of Britain's preserved railways becomes better known. A good car park is provided at Boat of Garten the easier end of the line from which to start the steam journey. At Aviemore there is no special parking, but of course many visitors will already be parked in one or other of the hotel complexes.

ABOVE Barclay 0–4–0 saddle tank.

BELOW Advertising signs at Boat of Garten station.

Address Strathspey Railway, The Station, Boat of Garten, Inverness, PH24 3BH. Tel. Boat of Garten 692

Enquiries to Above address. Timetable available

Opening times Mid-May to mid-October; Saturday and Sunday (May to October), Tuesday, Wednesday, Thursday (July and August)

How to get there *By road* to Boat of Garten ¾ mile off Aviemore-Grantown-on-Spey road (A95). Aviemore station is in Dalfaber Rd off A951 to Cairngorm. *By rail* to Aviemore BR

Facilities Car park and souvenir shop at Boat of Garten, refreshments on train

Discounts Special family rate, group reductions, children half-price

Scottish Railway Preservation Society

Preparations for steam at Falkirk.

Without as yet a run on tracks of its own, this Society possesses an excellent stock of locomotives and coaches covering a long period of Scottish railway history. A great deal of thought is being given to acquiring some track for regular steam operations. A line 1½ miles long to Bo'ness is likely to be revived with the help of the Scottish Tourist Board. In the meantime the Society is often able to run special trains over British Rail metals. It organizes excursions using its own historic rolling stock, even when motive power is diesel.

A visit to the Society's depot at Springfield Yard, Falkirk is very well worthwhile. Visitors are welcome almost every weekend. A nominal charge is made for admission, and frequently – especially in the summer months – engines will be seen in steam. On Bank Holidays steam is assured.

There are fourteen restored steam engines and six diesels, plus a collection of twenty coaches. Three of the latter are genuine Caledonian Railway vehicles, good solid bogies dating from 1921 which once formed part of the great expresses from Glasgow to Aberdeen. They, or at least two of them, sometimes journey far afield in Scotland on special trains, and at one time were regularly steam-hauled by the famous Caledonian 4–2–2 locomotive No. 123, last single driver in service.

Three of the engines preserved at Falkirk merit particular mention. One is the 4–4–0 former LNER express engine *Morayshire* (which appeared at the Rail 150 parade in County Durham in 1975). Another is *Maude*, a former North British 0–6–0 goods engine from 1891, for which donations were received from all over Scotland. The third is a traditional Caledonian 0–4–4 tank, once so familiar a sight on the Glasgow suburban lines. The diesels are small workhorses, three of them built by Ruston and Hornsby. The Society has one venerable engine most visitors want to see – the oldest Scottish built locomotive known to exist. She is a 0–4–0 well tank from Hawthorne of Leith dating from 1861, which worked for 96 years at a colliery in Lancashire.

Address Scottish Railway Preservation Society, Wallace St, Falkirk, FK2 7DR. Tel. Falkirk 20790

Enquiries to Above address. Programme of railtours available

Opening times All year, 11.00–17.00, Saturdays and Sundays. Steam, Easter and August Bank Holidays and some summer weekends

How to get there *By road* to Wallace St, off Grahams Rd, Falkirk. *By rail* to Falkirk Grahamston BR

Facilities Car park, refreshments and well-stocked souvenir shop

Discounts Family fares on certain excursion trips

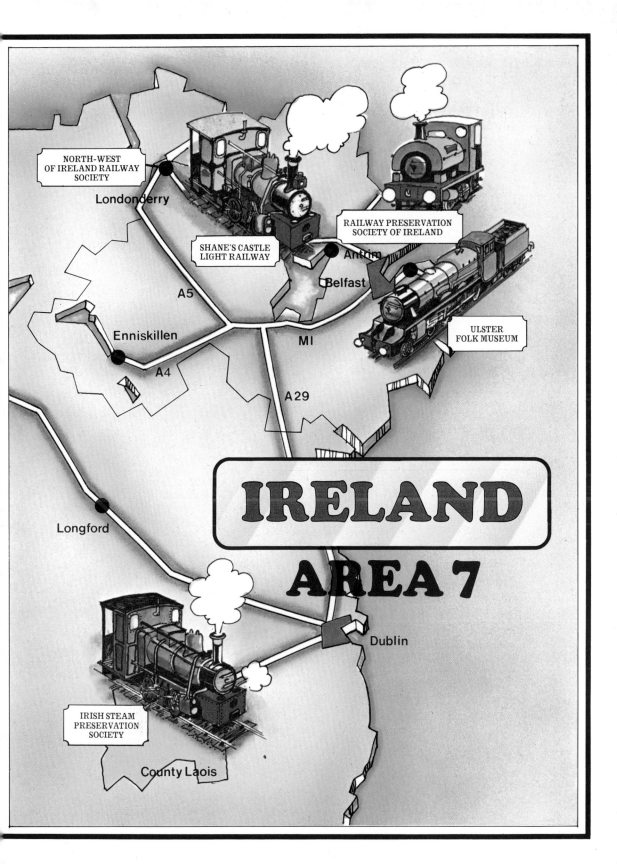

NORTH-WEST
OF IRELAND RAILWAY
SOCIETY

Londonderry

SHANE'S CASTLE
LIGHT RAILWAY

RAILWAY PRESERVATION
SOCIETY OF IRELAND

Antrim

Belfast

A5

Enniskillen

A4

M1

A29

ULSTER
FOLK MUSEUM

IRELAND

AREA 7

Longford

Dublin

IRISH STEAM
PRESERVATION
SOCIETY

County Laois

Introduction

Irish Steam Preservation Society

Railway preservation in Ireland is concentrated in the North, partly because that is where the coal is, and partly because there has been little interest in, or official encouragement for preservation in the Irish Republic. In consequence, some fascinating steam engines and delightful narrow gauge branch lines have been destroyed.

The unique Lartigue Monorail from Listowel to Ballybunion, where steam engines 'balanced' across a single rail, was among the lines lost. However, a few painstaking enthusiasts are working on an expensive reproduction, which may within two years allow visitors to sample a short stretch of this amazing railway.

Although the Railway Preservation Society of Ireland is based in Northern Ireland, it runs steam specials every year on both the NIR and CIE systems. The transport collection of the Ulster Folk Museum contains exhibits from all over Ireland.

Not to be confused with the Railway Preservation Society of Ireland, based in Ulster, this is mainly a narrow gauge scheme operating at Stradbally in Eire's County Laois. It has a 3 ft gauge line in the grounds of Stradbally Hall, which is being extended. On this there operates from time to time an Andrew Barclay 0–4–0 well tank dating from 1949 and a toast-rack type of carriage. The run is about $\frac{1}{2}$ mile at present and trips tend to be run on the first Sunday of each month in the summer.

In addition there is a museum of steam in the town of Stradbally, with three intriguing little engines, two of them of 1 ft 10 in gauge, the other (a Kennon 0–6–0 tender engine from 1955) working on a gauge one inch narrower. There is a 5 ft 3 in Drewry railcar on display, too.

Intending visitors should phone (see below) for an appointment to see over the museum and also to get details of any runs or steamings that may be taking place in the Hall grounds. The Society is closely involved with the National Steam Traction Engine Rally held early in August.

No. 3 *Shane* on Shane's Castle Light Railway.

Address Irish Steam Preservation Society Ltd, Stradbally, Co. Laois, Ireland. Tel. Stradbally 25136

Enquiries to The secretary at above address

Opening times May to October, 12.00–19.00 (approx.) for Traction Engine Rally dates, other dates as arranged. Trains tend to run first Sunday of each month in summer

How to get there *By road* 8 miles from Athy, 6 from Portlaoise. CIE bus from Dublin on Sundays only. *By rail* to Portlaoise

Facilities Car park, refreshments, and souvenir shop

Special attractions National Traction Engine Rally, early August. Steam Museum open by appointment

Discounts For groups, by arrangement. Children half-price

Ulster Folk and Transport Museum

All holders of rail tickets marked BCTMR and valid from Witham Street to Tamar Street walked that distance, because it was the foot journey between the entrance and exit of the former Belfast Transport Museum. This long, large red-brick building in East Belfast still houses splendid railway exhibits, but they are now part of the Ulster Folk and Transport Museum collection. A new site has been designated for rail transport with the Museum headquarters at Cultra, near Holywood, but it is unlikely to be developed for some years yet. In the mean time the exhibits will remain at Witham Street.

The star of the show does not belong to Northern Ireland at all. It is a Southern Irish express engine, the magnificent 4–6–0 *Maeve,* one of three quite short-lived locomotives built at Inchicore Works near Dublin in 1939 for working the Dublin-Cork mail trains.

Another most interesting vehicle is a horse-drawn 'dandy' (or double-decker tram trailer). It used, until 1957, to run the branch line traffic from the Great Northern of Ireland Railway's Fintona Junction to Fintona Town, just over half a mile. This was light track and the horse power was a saving over a steam engine. Connections were made with Belfast express trains stopping on their way from Enniskillen, and the tramway car carried first, second and third class passengers for its seven minute ride. It was not unique in the British Isles; a horse drawn dandy (now in York Museum) served the Port Carlisle branch until 1914.

The Irish gauge is 5 ft 3 in, although a good deal of narrower gauge existed in both North and South. Several steam locomotives of Northern Irish origin are in the Museum, including the popular GNR 4–4–0 *Merlin,* once a Belfast-Dublin express engine. There is an ex-GNR diesel railcar dating from 1934 (very early for this form of traction). The GNRI distinguished itself by using every form of traction on its lines over the years – steam, electric, battery, diesel, petrol, and horse! There is an older diesel railcar in the Museum – a 3 ft gauge unit built in 1932 for the Clogher Valley Light Railway.

Although the rail exhibits at Cultra are still at the planning stage, Cultra station, built in the 1860s, has recently been reopened.

Address Ulster Folk and Transport Museum, Witham St, Newtownards Rd, Belfast 4. Tel. Belfast 51519

Enquiries to Above address

Opening times Weekdays, 10.00–18.00

How to get there *By road* to East Belfast. *By rail* to Belfast NIR

CENTRE Ex-GNRI 4–4–0, part of the Ulster Folk and Transport Museum Collection.

BOTTOM The magnificent ex-CIE 4–6–0 Express *Maeve.*

Shane's Castle Light Railway

The only remaining narrow gauge steam operated railway in all Ireland, this line was built after all the others had closed. It was opened in 1971, is operated by the Lord O'Neill and runs from the outskirts of Antrim to the ruins of Old Shane's Castle, a distance of about 1½ miles. The gauge is 3 ft.

It is very popular, well advertised even in England, and attracts birdwatchers as well as railway enthusiasts, for it runs through woodlands that form part of a nature reserve.

There are two steam engines which undertake most of the work, a Peckett 0–4–0 tank and a Barclay 0–4–0 well tank named *Shane*. In reserve is a 0–6–0 tank not yet fully restored, plus two small works diesels. There are twelve coaches, four of them open four-wheelers used in good weather. Two goods trucks come from the

much-loved Londonderry and Lough Swilly Railway, which closed down more than a quarter of a century ago (although it survives as a bus and lorry company).

FAR RIGHT Barclay 0–4–0 well tank No. 3 *Shane.*

BELOW AND OPPOSITE Peckett 0–4–0 tank No. 1 *Tyrone,* built in 1904.

Address Shane's Castle Railway, Shane's Castle, Antrim, N. Ireland. Tel. Antrim 3380

Enquiries Estate Office, Shane's Castle, at above address. Tel. Antrim 2216. Timetable available

Opening times April to September, Sundays and Bank Holidays; June to August, Saturdays; July to August, Wednesdays, 12.00–18.00

How to get there *By road* A6 Antrim to Randalstown, through Antrim Gate Lodge. *By rail* to Antrim

Facilities Car park, refreshments and souvenir shop

Special attractions RSPB reserve, Nature Trail, children's playground, ruins of Shane's Castle, deer park

Discounts Children half-price

North-West of Ireland Railway Society

At one time the North-West of Ireland was covered by a network of narrow gauge steam railways, including the amazingly extensive County Donegal Railways and the Londonderry and Lough Swilly system. The Lough Swilly's Burtonport line was 49 miles in length, making a narrow gauge run of $63\frac{1}{2}$ miles from Londonderry, while the Donegal Railways had two runs of some 50 miles. Nothing remains except some rotting County Donegal rolling stock in store at Strabane. This was purchased many years ago by an American, but no move was made to transport it to his New Jersey estate. The collection is reported seriously vandalized.

The Railway Society was formed to restore a mile of the system from Londonderry (Victoria Road) to Riverside Park. It was possible to operate a partly restored County Donegal Railways diesel railcar over a distance of 150 yards. The NWIRS has two Nasmyth Wilson 2–6–4 tanks from 1907, two railcars, a composite coach and some underframes.

However, as there is now a threat to sell the station, much of the stock has been moved to Shane's Castle. To be successful in rail restoration a large and interested population within a 50 mile radius is essential, and calm conditions. These do not exist at present to a sufficient extent in troubled West Ulster and Donegal.

Address North-West of Ireland Railway Society, Londonderry (Victoria Rd) Station, N. Ireland. Tel. Londonderry 44776
Enquiries to K. Thompson, 64 Prenen Park, Londonderry, N. Ireland

Opening times Check with Society for details

Facilities Car park and souvenir shop

How to get there *By road* A2 or A5 to Londonderry. *By rail* to Londonderry NIR station, then bus

Railway Preservation Society of Ireland

Based at Whitehead excursion station a few miles from Belfast, this large and enthusiastic body is dedicated to the saving of relics of Irish railways and running tours with its own engines and rolling stock over lengths of the Irish system. It is perhaps better known for the tours it runs to extant steam systems abroad, working with Williames Travel of Belfast (whose Managing Director Mr Ian Slaughter is an active officer). Its tours to the railways of India have become well established. The Lord O'Neill is President of the Preservation Society, a noted landowner with his own railway (see Shane's Castle Light Railway, see page 148).

The Society carries out its own minor repairs at Whitehead on its half dozen steam engines and around a dozen varied passenger coaches. It does not need a line of its own for short runs, for no restrictions are placed by either Northern Ireland Railways or the CIE of Eire on the use of steam specials. As a result, the Society's trains range the length and breadth of Ireland on certain well publicized and heavily supported occasions. Often the trains are double-headed with ex-GNR 4–4–0 *Slieve Gullion* heading 2–6–4 tank No. 4 from the NCC, or a J15 0–6–0 dating from 1879.

Less likely to be active is the fascinating former Sligo, Leitrim and Northern Counties 0–6–4 tank *Lough Erne,* but a former Guinness industrial saddle tank goes out on the track at Whitehead to give short rides.

Among the many items of rolling stock, much of which goes out on long distance runs, is a dining car from the GNR built in 1938. There is also a twelve-wheeled brake/composite coach which once formed part of the *Rosslare Express* out of Dublin in Edwardian days, and the GNR Directors Saloon from 1911.

'Split engine' tours have been pioneered by the Preservation Society in recent years, which have proved highly successful. A double-headed train is divided somewhere en route, and joins up later for the run home. Any visitors to Ireland should watch the press for announcements for these tours, for they give a perfectly reproduced picture of Irish rail travel in the steam age.

Jeep 2–6–4 tank at Whitehead.

Address Railway Preservation Society of Ireland, Excursion Station, Whitehead, Co. Antrim, N. Ireland

Enquiries to Above address

Opening times Steaming days all over Ireland. Local runs on Sunday afternoons in July and August

How to get there *By road* A2 to Whitehead. *By rail* to Whitehead

Facilities Car park, refreshments and souvenir shop

British Rail's Scenic Lines

While few commuters find pleasure in the daily railway journey, there are several holiday train routes which delight all passengers, and most business travellers, riding first class on high speed trains or overnight in comfortable sleepers, must regard their journeys as pleasurable.

British Rail, having decided to 'get in on the act' with steam operations (see page 16) now runs scheduled steam services on summer weekends, using locomotives supplied by the best Sheds in private hands, notably Steamtown Carnforth, or engines on loan from the National Museum at York. The routes served by steam under the British Rail banner are from Leeds to Harrogate and from Carnforth to Barrow-in-Furness and on to Ravenglass. An excellent feature of these trains is that fares are held to more or less the normal charged for conventional diesel runs over the same route.

There are some British Rail routes which qualify as journeys for pleasure, on which passengers may be riding a train for the scenery alone. Four of them are singled out for special mention, all diesel lines and all exceptionally scenic. Obviously all four routes have regular passengers, including a few who may not even lift their heads from newspapers or books throughout the journey but, in summer time at least, the majority of riders will be watching out of the window.

The routes are the West Highland Line (Glasgow Queen Street to Oban, Fort William and Mallaig), the Skye Line (from Inverness to Kyle of Lochalsh), the Cambrian Coast Line (Shrewsbury to Aberystwyth and Dovey Junction to Pwllheli), and the 'Long Drag' (the Settle and Carlisle). The Cambrian Coast Line has the added attraction that it links together most of the 'Great Little Trains of Wales', a factor of great importance to their continued survival in the years ahead as fuel supplies become scarce and expensive and motor car traffic begins to dwindle.

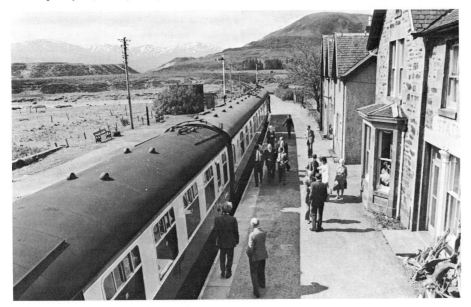

Achnasheen Station on the Inverness to Kyle of Lochalsh Line.

West Highland Line

This magnificent route has captivated travellers for 80 years. It is one of the few sections of railway for which British Rail issue a guide free of charge to passengers. It is called 'A Line for All Seasons' and is published by the Scottish Region in Glasgow.

Starting from Queen Street Station with its elegant roof and fanlight, trains climb through a dismal and very dank tunnel to Cowlairs, but once emerged into daylight they are clear of the least attractive parts of the city and running through Maryhill Park to Westerton soon to be joined with the electric suburban line which runs close to the Clyde on its way to Dumbarton. The great Rock of Dumbarton is seen before the Clyde widens and the trains swings northwards, past Helensburgh and up between Loch Lomond and, first, the Gareloch where at Faslane great wartime convoys assembled and now nuclear submarines lie, then Loch Long. There is a stop at Arrochar and Tarbet, twin villages, one on Loch Lomond the other on Loch Long, and then comes Ardlui, at the head of Lomond.

To quote from British Rail's guide to the Line, 'the route taken was determined by engineering considerations, not by any requirement that it should pass through areas of great natural beauty, but if the planners had decided that it was to be primarily a scenic line, then it is difficult to see how the route would have been any different from the one selected – for there is no more delightful journey in Britain than this'.

It beats the road journey at all points, for often the rails are clinging high up on a mountainside with the road (where it exists at all) lying deep in a valley. Once up on Rannoch Moor and crossing it, there is no road and even a school is on a station platform! The line to Fort William was opened in 1894, and the extension to Mallaig in 1901. The former was contracted by Formans & McCall of Glasgow and the latter by Robert McAlpine's, for the North British Railway Company.

Before the climb to Rannoch Moor and soon after leaving Crianlarich, most important of the intermediate stations between Helensburgh and Fort William, the line divides. One branch strikes due westwards, passing along the shores of Loch Awe, through deep gorges over the Pass of Brander, and then to Connel Ferry (nearest station to Glencoe) before running alongside Loch Etive and zig-zagging down Glen Cruitten to the town and resort of Oban. The Oban line was part of the Caledonian Railway Company.

The West Highland Line proper continues by way of Tyndrum (Upper) to Bridge of Orchy then on to the wild Rannoch Moor. A viaduct on a horseshoe curve below Ben Douran (3523ft) between Tyndrum (Upper) and Bridge of Orchy is a superbly scenic stretch of track, frequently photographed. Four mountains (Ben a Dthaidh, Ben Mhanach, Ben Achadh, and Ben a Chreachain) dominate the eastern part of the Moor, all of them well over 3000ft.

The train descends from Rannoch Moor through Corrour and beside Loch Treign, over the River Spean viaduct near Tulloch station and with the Spean rushing alongside the tracks passes through Roy Bridge. Over to the left may be seen the Monessie Gorge. As the train curves around to reach Fort William the great mass of Ben Nevis, 4406ft and the highest mountain in the British Isles, is always in view, flanked by only slightly lesser heights, Aonach Beag at 4060ft and Aonach Mor, exactly 4000ft.

Fort William is a terminus, and trains reverse direction here before striking north and west for Mallaig. Some people reckon the final 42 miles on to Mallaig to be the most scenic of the whole route, largely due to the sea lochs and beaches to the left of the down train (bound for Mallaig). Loch Eil is in view for a long time, and at Glenfinnan, Loch Shiel may be seen, also Prince Charlie's monument. The Long Glenfinnan Viaduct is the most dramatic on the entire West Highland System. Loch Eilt parallels the tracks on the right hand side for several miles before Lochailort station, where the Loch of that name is in view. A number of short tunnels occur between Lochailort and Arisaig, where Loch Nan Ceall reaches inland. The Sound of Sleat appears as the train crosses the River Morar with its white sands and enters the fishing and ferry port of Mallaig on Glasnacardoch Bay.

Years ago, special observation saloons were attached to trains on the West Highland and Oban lines, which proved very popular even with a supplementary fare. However, they eventually wore out and in the years of austerity no replacements were planned. Mallaig was the last terminus to handle a rear-end observation car. However, a car has now been provided for the Skye Line (see page 154).

Mallaig is the embarkation port for three ferries, to Armadale in Skye (this one takes cars), one to the 'cocktail islands' of Eigg, Muck, Rhum and Canna, and the third to Kyle of Lochalsh where a connection is made with the splendid Kyle to Inverness railway (The Skye Line).

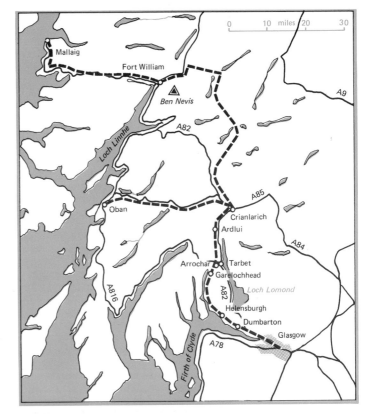

The West Highland Line near Tyndrum.

153

Skye Line
(Inverness to Kyle of Lochalsh)

This beautiful route leaves the Highland main line from Inverness to Wick at Dingwall, 19 miles from Inverness (known throughout the world as the 'Highland Capital'). Built as the Dingle and Skye Railway it was opened to Strome Ferry in 1870, this sea-loch harbour serving as base for ferries to Skye for some 27 years until the extension to Kyle of Lochalsh was constructed (with great difficulty through rocky terrain) in 1897.

The Highland Railway Company was formed by mergers in 1865 so that it was under Highland auspices that both these routes into the virtually unknown 'Wester Ross' territory were completed. It was said in the House of Lords at the time of the great railway construction into North-West Scotland (the West Highland and the Skye Line extension) that 'until the coming of the railways and the engineers building them, the British public knew as little about these remote areas as the geographers did about Central Africa twenty years before'.

Certainly the line traverses wild country, but it is beautiful and lonely, with sparse habitation. There are no great heights to climb, the attraction of the scenery being the water, heather, and distant highland. Beyond Strome Ferry it is like travelling beside a Norwegian Fjord.

From Dingwall to the terminus at Kyle, built onto the waters of the Sound of Sleat, is fractionally under 64 miles, the whole distance from Inverness being 83 miles. The first 19 miles to Dingwall are pleasant enough, with views of Clachnaharry and glimpses of the northern end of Loch Ness, followed later by fine panoramas of Beauly Firth, the sunniest region in Scotland. The Black Isle, lying on the northern side of Beauly, has the most fertile soil in Scotland.

Junctioning westwards at Dingwall, the Skye Line runs for many miles under the long, looming brow of Ben Wyvis, climbing gently and soon in view of Strathpeffer Spa, once a highly popular watering place. There used to be a branch line from Dingwall to a terminus at the Spa which, 70 years ago, had a dozen trains a day on a push–pull operation.

The Skye Line climbs to Raven Rock Summit on a grade of 1 in 50, so it is slow going even for diesel locomotives. There are descents which compensate although speed limits have to be enforced. Frequently sheep get on the line and occasionally get killed. Garve station is a roadhead for Ullapool and Loch Broom; this was the base for one of Britain's last horse-drawn stage coach routes, which ran until the late 1920s. At Achnasheen, where once the restaurant car on the westbound train was detached and hooked on to the eastbound train, there is another road link, this one going to Aultbea, Poolewe (famed for the most northerly sub-tropical gardens) and Loch Ewe, much used during the Second World War as a convoy base. This, too, was stage-coach served until the late 1920s.

The route now lies to the south-west, with splendid views of Wester Ross and the mountains aroud Loch Torridon. It is a descent along Strath Carron to the Achnashellach Forest, and then to the head of the great sea loch, Carron, the train clinging to its southern shore for several miles until Strome Ferry is reached. Here the evidence remains of the once busy harbour which used to see Highland Railway steamers sailing to Portree and even to Stornoway. One vessel, the *Ferret*, was actually stolen from this port under the guise of a charter and was not recovered until it had reached Melbourne, Australia!

The Kyle Extension is taken through very difficult country, clinging to a rocky ledge above the waters of Loch Carron, past the village of Plockton and round the coast with magnificent maritime views until Kyle of Lochalsh comes into sight some three hours after leaving Inverness. The Port has been described as a 'Highland Fishguard', paying tribute to the Great Western Railway engineers who dug their

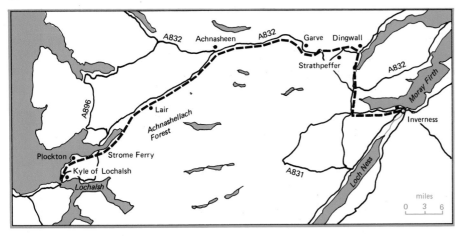

way through rock to open up the West Wales port. There are three trains each way daily on the Skye Line, the 10.30 from Inverness carrying an observation saloon on loan to BR from Flying Scotsman Enterprises. This train also has a buffet car. Both cars return from Kyle with the 17.55 train, but the observation saloon only runs from May to September on Mondays, Wednesdays and Fridays.

Cambrian Coast Line

Not long ago, through express trains from London (Paddington) and Manchester ran to the popular Welsh coastal resorts of Aberystwyth and Pwllheli. Since re-organisation, the Cambrian Coast route has been under constant threat of closure, and its services are cut back to provide six round trips a day from Shrewsbury to Machynlleth, where the multiple unit diesels divide, one section going to Pwllheli, the other to Aberystwyth. Only on summer Saturdays are there through trains to the latter resort from Manchester and the North, but they are all year round to Wolverhampton.

Because of track damage by gales and falling rocks, the cost of upkeep is admittedly high, but support for the line is growing. It provides an essential link between six of the 'Great Little Trains of Wales'. Welshpool station serves the Welshpool and Llanfair (by way of a short bus ride to Raven Square); Aberystwyth is itself the station for the BR-worked Vale of Rheidol line; Tywyn is terminus for the Talyllyn Railway; Fairbourne Station is a stone's throw from the popular little 15in

gauge Fairbourne Railway taking holiday-makers to the Estuary; Porthmadog is terminus for the Festiniog and for the newly restored section of the Welsh Highland Railway.

Journeys begin at Shrewsbury, a magnificent pseudo-Tudor station in the shadow of Shrewsbury Castle. This is still a busy place, with train services in six directions. The Cambrian trains leave heading due west into the Shropshire hills before turning southwards to cross the fledgling River Severn at Welshpool, 19 miles from Shrewsbury.

Leaving Welshpool there is a view of massive Powys Castle to the right, a gigantic Marches fortress still completely intact. The line soon enters the Upper Severn Valley and follows it to Newtown, a surprisingly large town, and then strikes away northwestwards across high country to Caersws and Talerddig before entering the Dovey Valley. There is a stop at the pleasant town of Machynlleth, where the multiple unit divides although the routes do not separate until Dovey Junction about 3 miles beyond.

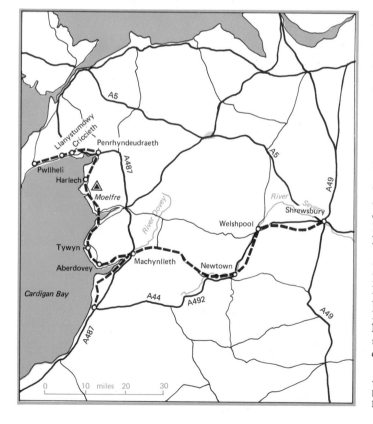

The Aberystwyth train keeps to the southern side of the Dovey Valley and its widening estuary, reaches the shores of Cardigan Bay, passes through the unusually named Bow Street and terminates at Aberystwyth station, a place of faded Great Western elegance. It is $81\frac{1}{2}$ miles from Shrewsbury.

The second section of the train which set out from Shrewsbury follows a much longer and more scenic route to reach Pwllheli. From Dovey Junction it keeps close to the northern shore of the widening estuary to Aberdovey, then heads due north to Tywyn (Talyllyn Railway). Attaining the shores of Cardigan Bay at Aber Dysynni Point it clings to the sea for many miles to Fairbourne, with fine mountain views to the right.

At Fairbourne, where the miniature line goes off to the golf links, sands, and ferry, the Cambrian Coast Line goes inland a little way and then crosses the very wide estuary of the Mawddach by a long bridge, a crossing not possible by road, for the road bridge requires a long drive upstream all the way to Penmaenpool. The Cambrian Coast Line's great distance advantage has long been a factor in keeping it going.

Again the direction reverts to due north, at first along the shore and then inland past Talybont and Dyffryn along the lower slopes of Moelfre (1943 ft). The shore is reached again at Llandanwg and held as far as Harlech, where the dramatic castle is such a landmark. The train has now got as far as the top end of Cardigan Bay, called at this point Tremadog Bay. It swings inland in a northeasterly direction for 5 miles to the edge of Snowdonia, then turns due west at Penrhyndeudraeth close to the line of the Festiniog Railway which it actually crosses at Minfford (the stations of both lines are very close) before running downhill into Porthmadog.

There is still quite a distance to go along the Lleyn Peninsula at the top of Tremadog Bay, through Criccieth, but the scenery is less dramatic. Between Llanystumdwy and the terminus at Pwllheli a large Butlins Holiday Camp can be seen on the sands at Penychain. The ride ends virtually on the seacoast after 119 miles from Shrewsbury, covered in approximately 4 hours.

TOP The Cambrian Coast line alongside the Dovey Estuary.

Settle and Carlisle Line

Building the 'Long Drag' over the Pennines in 1870–76 was the last great work on a main line railway undertaken in conventional style by armies of navvies. It was a tremendous task, largely through inhospitable country which in winter was cruel above the thousand foot level. The Midland Railway sought to provide itself with a route to Scotland, becoming the third competitor for the lucrative Anglo-Scottish traffic with the special emphasis on tapping the big cities of the Midlands.

As men toiled over the high moors they created some of the finest viaducts the world has ever known. Tunnels and earthworks were built to the highest standards and the main line became one of the best ever laid. The summit, at Ais Gill, under the shadow of Boar Fell, is 1189 ft above sea level, the loftiest of any main or secondary line in England. The signal box there is 6 miles from a village.

Books about the Settle and Carlisle Railway, including one by Mitchell and Joy published in 1966, give an insight into the Victorian engineers and workmen who undertook the task of forcing a great main line over the hills and moors of the loneliest and wildest part of England.

The toll of human life on the Settle–Carlisle was considerable, an average of one man lost every week for five years. At Chapel-le-Dale cemetery there are the graves of over 100 navvies. Severe winters

The eleven arch Arten Gill Viaduct on the Settle and Carlisle Line.

157

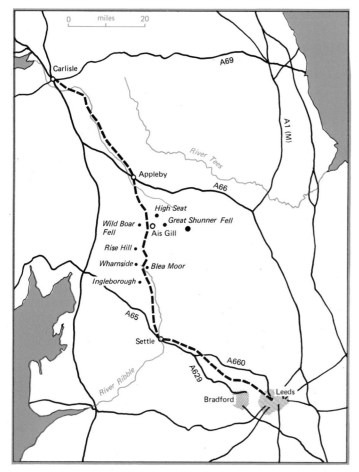

enthusiasts' specials, and as many as 10 steam trains will run each way during a season. Only 15 miles from Leeds is Keighley, station for the famous preservation line Keighley and Worth Valley Railway.

The normal diesel service over 'the Long Drag' tends to be sparse these days, now that through trains such as the St. Pancras–Glasgow 'Thames–Clyde Express' and St. Pancras–Edinburgh 'Thames–Forth Express' no longer operate. It is limited to three Nottingham and Sheffield to Carlisle buffet car trains in each direction on weekdays and one each way on Sundays. There are eight each way as far as Skipton, most of these branching off for Morecambe.

The Pennine route to Carlisle from Leeds is a journey which everyone at all interested in railways should make, regardless of traction or even the time of year. If the opportunity presents itself of getting on a steam special, it should be grasped eagerly. The railway will soon prove to any 'doubting Thomas' that there are still plenty of open spaces in England.

The section from Settle Junction to Appleby provides the greatest scenic thrills and engineering wonders. In these 44 miles are crammed more magnificent viaducts and heavy earthworks than any comparable distance in Britain. Ribblehead Viaduct is the finest of them all, but Dent Head Viaduct, Dandry Mire Viaduct (700 ft long), the eleven arch Arten Gill Viaduct, Crosby Gill Viaduct, and Ormside Viaduct are worth watching for, although the best views are naturally not from the train but a mile away on the moors.

The windswept summits of the Pennines to watch for include Pen-y-ghent (2273 ft), Wild Boar Fell, Ingleborough, Whernside (2419 ft), Rise Hill near Dent (1825 ft but the train is already two-thirds of the way up this mountain), Great Shunner Fell (2340 ft), and High Seat.

Descending from Ais Gill to Appleby and beyond, the railway is in the Eden Valley and the country gradually becomes more friendly and pastoral. The River Eden is crossed several times on the way down to Carlisle. Trains from Carlisle to Leeds descending from Ais Gill southwards pick up the Ribble Valley at Ribblehead and stay close to the river as far as Hellifield. Soon after that the railway enters Airedale, and remains with it nearly all the way to Leeds.

block the lines and accidents have occurred periodically. The term 'Long Drag' originally referred to the climb from Settle Junction (where the branch to Carnforth and Morecambe goes off) to Blea Moor Tunnel, 17 miles with long stretches at a gradient of 1 in 100, but in fact it is now applied to the entire railway. Up trains have a 'long drag' in front of them when coming from Appleby to Ais Gill Summit, about 18 miles with many lengths of 1 in 100. The Settle and Carlisle line is above the thousand foot mark for more than 20 miles, from Horton-in-Ribblesdale to near Kirkby Stephen.

Trains for Carlisle by this former Midland route start at Leeds, and the length of the run is 114 miles. It was always a great test of steam locomotives especially in the days of small engines. Today, it is an authorized route for steam workings on

Alphabetical list of entries

(Key numbers to map on page 8 appear in brackets)